Mom

ON A MISSION

Mom
ON A MISSION

UNLEASHING YOUR WARRIOR HEART

BY STEFANI STOLTZFUS

www.wallsofhome.com

stefani@wallsofhome.com

www.facebook.com/groups/battlefieldmoms

ISBN-13: 978-1986320689

ISBN-10: 1986320685

*This book is dedicated first of all to Jesus,
the Author and Finisher of our faith.
Every word is written for His glory.*

*To moms everywhere who are striving to
raise their children for the Kingdom of Christ.*

Table of Contents

Introduction

They were a small, insignificant looking band: four young children, walking through the deep forest, following their leader. Their leader was a young woman, average to look at, except for one thing. Over her dress she wore a breastplate, in her right hand she held a sword and in her left, a massive shield. Because she was on a mission.

She knew the children placed in her charge were neither insignificant, nor ordinary. Deep in their packs they each carried a treasure of infinite worth, and it was her job to protect it — and them. The children were mostly unaware of their worth, which gave them a sweet innocence, but it also made them vulnerable.

Although the path they walked on looked safe, their leader knew there would be many along the way who would love nothing more than to entice the children away from it, away from the castle she was leading them towards. The treasure they carried would not only be useful to the enemy, the loss of it would be a blow to the King. So she kept her sword close and her shield ready.

They came to a small village where they stopped at a tavern for refreshment. The children happily chattered among themselves and with the young woman while they waited for their food. The tavern owner came to their table with a large goblet, full of a delicious looking drink, which he offered to the children, free of charge. He tried to give it directly to one of the young boys, but the woman intercepted him and took the goblet herself. It took only a small taste for her to know it was unacceptable for those in her charge. She sent it back, despite the eager remonstrance of the innkeeper.

The children were bitterly disappointed – they were so ready for the taste of something besides water. The young woman quieted them and explained that although the drink was good to look at and pleasant to drink, it was tainted with a potion that would gradually take control of their minds and destroy their ability to judge anything rightly.

They soon finished their meal and continued their journey. They came by a man in the town square who was in the middle of an entertaining act. The children wanted so badly to stay and watch that the woman relented. As the act went on, it drew her in. She momentarily forgot the possible danger to the children as she let her mind wander. Someone jostled against her, and she was quickly brought back to reality as she saw a strange woman pulling one of the little girls after her. She quickly drew her sword, which rested in its scabbard, and the enemy retreated in fear and disgust. She was shaken by the encounter and resolved to not be so easily distracted in the future.

As they left the town behind them, she held the sword firmly in her hand once again, and her shield was ready to protect the children from any onslaughts of the enemy. She was exhausted at times, but learned to draw her strength from the words of the King and the life-giving water with which He always gave her in good supply, whenever she needed it.

They met many perils and were tempted with many deceptions along the way - in the forests and the towns. But she kept her eyes on the goal ahead. As the children grew older, she told them stories of the mighty King, and they learned to love Him. She taught them how to use the sword and shield, along with other weapons that He had given them.

And so they went on, the woman who was growing and maturing in her heart, and the children who were fast on their way to becoming adults and warriors in their own right. She knew they would soon be out of her charge. She could only lead them safely for so long, then the journey was their own choice. They could go on to the castle, or pursue the empty pleasures that their enemies made look so enticing.

She battled for them fearlessly, without thought of herself. She spent much time teaching them about the treasure they were carrying, the battle all around them and the words of the King. And she hoped what she taught them would be enough.

This is a simple allegory, but the truth is powerful. Mom, you are that young woman, trusted with the precious souls of your children. We only have a short season to be with our children, and it is absolutely critical that we use that time to protect, fight for and prepare them to become warriors themselves.

Now I know from experience that this can be an abstract concept. It's hard to pin down exactly what it means to be a "Warrior Mom." When we are in the trenches, surviving the day to day struggles of parenting, it's so tempting to just go with the minimum. But God has called us to rise above the everyday and sound the battle cry loud and clear! It's not enough to fight when we are being attacked; we need to take an offensive position and lead our little tribes with grace, courage and valor.

It's a journey that will not end anytime soon, and we can put away the fear of imperfection right now. Being a warrior does not mean being perfect – all you really need is ready obedience and a heart after God. I have waited so long for my Christian walk to be more perfect before answering God's call to truly be a Warrior Mom, but I am learning that growth comes best when I am practicing *what I know* instead of waiting for God to shower inspiration and growth on my heart.

I believe there are two important parts to becoming a Warrior Mom, and that's what I want to share with you in this book. The first part is the boot camp. No soldier will reach their full potential without training, not even a warrior of God. It is in God's boot camp that we learn who we really are. The second essential to becoming battle worthy is learning to step into the identity that God created for us as moms and claiming the power we have through His might.

I must warn you before you start: our enemy does not want you to learn how to battle for your children. He does not want you to become a warrior or to claim your identity as a member of God's army. Watch out for his attacks and distractions, and be on the offensive, covering yourself and your family in prayer.

Part 1: Who She Is

"He teaches my hands to make war, so
That my arms can bend a bow of bronze."
—2 Samuel 22:35

chapter one

Broken for a Purpose

"Whenever God means to make a man great,
He always breaks him in pieces first."
— Charles Spurgeon[1]

She was perfect. We stared down at her in awe, holding our breath until we could hold her for the first time. The moment we saw her, we knew. We knew she was our daughter, perfectly created for our hearts and made for our family. We had waited two years for this moment. Two years of paperwork, appointments and home visits. Two years full of soaring hopes and crashing dreams. Adoption can be like a brutal boot camp for the faint of heart.

But now, here she was: our precious Mila baby. And we were on cloud nine. The hospital gave us our own room for the three day stay while we waited for paperwork to be signed and our daughter to be released *to us*. Then the nurses came into our room around midnight, just twelve hours before she was due to be released. Words swirled around like in a bad dream, and before we knew it, our baby was out of our arms and in the NICU, enduring blood draws and a spinal tap. We were heartbroken.

After a few days everything was starting to feel okay again. My heart almost broke in two when our baby's precious first mom told Mila goodbye and put her in my arms before walking out of the hospital. She had signed her parenting rights over to us, and I felt shattered on the inside for her, because my dreams came true through her bleeding heart. But our little girl was going to be ok. We just needed to hang tight at the

NICU for another week, and then we would hopefully have the go-ahead to return home.

But then another late night was shattered by a single phone call. Suddenly nothing was clear. An unforeseen legal complication had come up and there was nothing we could do. It is impossible to describe the shattered, ragged, bleeding feeling of knowing your newborn daughter might be taken from you and given to another. My husband and I felt like we were thrown into the middle of a tornado, with our hearts being twisted, bruised and tossed in all directions.

We clung to God and to each other tighter than ever before, and in that brokenness, I learned how weak and helpless I am apart from God's strength and that He is the only one who can hold together my broken pieces without destroying my heart. It was as if God was holding me on a mountain top as I watched the swirling storm below, myself a part of it, yet so far removed.

And I learned to know God in a way I never had before. I saw my raw need for Him and looked at my pride with a broken and contrite heart. You see, I'd always been so confident in my ability. I'd done things and been places. I'd devoured Christian books and gone to church and traveled to many different countries. I'd bandaged up hurt people and helped resuscitate when there was no life left. I was confident in my ability to fix things, yet there I was, totally broken and unable to fix anything.

The purpose

It is only when God knocks all the props out from under us that we realize who we are. *We are nothing without Him.* And I started to think. Maybe being a warrior mom isn't about winning battles because we fight through with our own sheer determination. Maybe it's God winning our battles as He takes us on a journey that will equip us beyond motherhood. For that journey, He has given us a map, a blueprint if you will.

There was a time when the children of Israel were living the dream in Egypt. A member of their family was second in command over the entire country, perhaps even over the known world at the time. Pharaoh gave them their own land, the best in the country, and they were offered high-ranking jobs. God had saved them from the famine, and they were grateful. Things looked good, and they were feeling great.

And then the storm came and their lives came crashing down around their feet. They went from positions of privilege to slavery. And then, as if that wasn't bad enough, their baby boys were ripped out of their arms and thrown into the river. They were broken, shattered into a million pieces. But God…God had not forgotten them and was waiting to show Himself mighty on their behalf. He rescued them from slavery and obliterated their enemies. He worked miracle after miracle for them, fulfilling every promise and making new covenants with them. But it was not until He took them on a journey, fighting their battles for them while gently leading them along, that they became warriors.

First things first

My friend, it's going to be the same for each of us. We cannot wake up one morning and decide we are going to go to battle for our children, and voila! We have instantly become seasoned, strong warrior women ready to fight hard with grace and fire in our hearts. First, we must go on the journey. We must learn to rely on God with every fiber of our being and learn what it is to be broken, repentant, reliant and vulnerable before we can then be bold and victorious.

I believe the path to becoming a warrior woman usually goes in that order, but God is not bound by any particular five step method, so this will not always be the case. But since this is the path we observe the

Israelites took, I'd like to discuss our path in that same order: brokenness before victory.

Have you ever been broken? Some of us are harder than others, and it takes more to break us. Others have such gentle hearts toward the Lord that it doesn't take much. It took rejection, almost losing our baby and a long, hard transition as a mom of three kids to completely shatter me. But don't expect your path to look like mine. One of the biggest keys to the entire journey is to not compare your path with those around you. You are unique as an individual, a Christian and a mom, so God's way for you will be equally unique.

Being broken hurts from the inside out. It's the kind of pain that those around you only catch glimpses of. The most painful part is hidden way down, deep inside. Brokenness is feeling misunderstood and unknown. It is God taking a red hot iron and probing the most sensitive parts of us, purging out self and leaving only scars behind. It is God's grace, like a small plant, growing larger and larger inside of us, until our carefully constructed walls of self-sufficiency are forced to shatter into a thousand pieces, leaving us feeling vulnerable and exposed.

Brokenness can be as simple as acknowledging our own silly, useless pride for what it is: embarrassing, ugly and revolting. Something that needs to be killed. And because we have identified with our pride for so long, it will not die without pain. You will feel like a piece of yourself is dying.

But to be truly broken we must allow the pain to do its work, breaking our identity away from our own accomplishments and uniting it with Christ. When the Israelites left Egypt, the Egyptians and surrounding nations weren't talking about them as slaves who built the pyramids. They had a new identity: The children of the great I AM. God had a plan for them as a nation. He was going to bring salvation to the world through them. But first, they had to have their own identity smashed so that everyone would know they belonged to Him. No longer were they the slaves of the Egyptians; they were the people of the Living God.

This is what He wants for us as mothers. He doesn't want us to raise children that make people look at us. He wants us to raise children that point people to Him. And to do that, He must break us and rebuild us with His own identity.

Journey not destination

Brokenness, however, is not a destination, but a journey. It is something we have to say "yes" to over and over again. In fact, there are times we need to beg and plead for God to break us and replace the broken pieces with Himself. Brokenness is not something we experience once and then we're good to go. It is an attitude of the heart that goes deeper and deeper over time.

Imagine your heart as an onion, with layer after layer. God doesn't want just the top layer or two. He wants to get right to the center so that every inch of us is filled with Him. But He starts with the outer shell, peeling back layer after layer over the years of our lives until He finally reaches the most protected parts of our souls.

So expect to be on the mountaintop with God during your brokenness, but don't expect to stay there. Our frail human hearts run down to the valley of self so easily, building the walls of pride and self-defense up again and again. We find it easy to feel invincible after we've been on the mountaintop. So we must plead with God to break us again and again, until we can live in an attitude of continual, humble brokenness before Him.

If we are not willing to beg, plead and embrace brokenness, then the battle is already lost. The brutal truth is that we are unable to effectively fight in our own power. In fact, if we live with our walls of pride built up around us, we are blocking God's power from our lives. But when we invite brokenness then we are inviting God's glorious power to show itself strong in us. And I imagine God beckoning us closer as He says "Now you shall see what I will do" (Exodus 6:1).

Are you ready to see the glory of the Lord?

Read Psalm 105 and write down the 3 times God showed Himself strong and brought life after brokenness.

_____

_____

_____

_____

Have you ever felt shattered?

_____

What was it that broke through to your heart?

_____

_____

_____

_____

How are you able to see God's grace in those hard circumstances?

_____

_____

_____

_____

"But may the God of all grace, who called us to His eternal glory by
Christ Jesus, after you have suffered a while, perfect, establish,
strengthen, and settle you."
—1 Peter 5:10

chapter two

Walking in Obedience

"But be doers of the word, and not
Hearers only, deceiving yourselves."
—James 1:22

During the summer I like to go on walks with the kids. It doesn't happen very often, but when it does, it's a great time to listen to what's on their minds and observe different plants and little animals along the way. Almost every time we go on a walk, we end up playing the "stop game." We'll be walking and talking, and I'll randomly tell them to stop. They are supposed to stop right where they are and not move a muscle until I tell them to go again.

Just a simple, fun game, right? Well the truth is, I have a strong motive behind it. We live in an area known for its rattlesnakes. In fact, a friend just told me their neighbor girl has been bitten twice. Another friend had a dog get bit. This is a big deal to me. In the case that we would run into a rattlesnake during our walks or any other time, my kid's instant obedience would be crucial to their safety and well-being.

Our obedience to God is just as crucial to our spiritual well-being, and it is the second installment of His boot camp. Any soldier worthy of the name knows that obedience is not an option, but a requirement. We rely on the wisdom, experience and knowledge of our Commanding Officer for our safety and our advance against the enemy. A soldier does not always know all the details behind the order but must trust the one above him *with his life.*

If we go back to the children of Israel during their exodus from Egypt, we can learn some important things. Their blind, trusting obedience to God saved their sons from certain death. Through their obedience, they plundered the wealth of the Egyptians without lifting a finger against them. And ultimately, their obedience brought them *freedom*. Leaving Egypt may have been exciting, but it was still a big unknown (Exodus 12).

Their faith was stretched and tested in the most rigorous ways. And then God tested them more. Imagine this: they were finally on their way out of the land that had held them captive for 430 years. *430 years, y'all.* That's a long time. They must have been bubbling over with praise, rejoicing in the greatness of God.

But suddenly, in the midst of their rejoicing, they see a cloud of dust rising in the distance behind them. It doesn't take long for them to figure out they are being pursued by the whole Egyptian army! They ran to Moses, terrified, their fear flowing over into accusations. But then the message comes from God: "Be still. I will fight for you and you can just be still."

I imagine that was one of the hardest commands to obey. The men wanted to fight for their families! The women wanted to save their babies. Every fiber in their beings must have felt the need to flee or fight, but God told them to be still. And because obedience builds on obedience, they were able to listen. God had slowly grown their faith in Him, miracle after miracle, command after command, until they knew they could trust Him.

And friend, He will do the same for you. Obedience is not something to be feared. We can embrace the commands of God because He has proven Himself *to be good.* He is good! He has shown us His Father's heart for us. He tells us He has a plan for us, and it is for our future.

Obedience is like brokenness in many ways. We need to ask God to give us a spirit of obedience and the willingness to go wherever He calls. And it is not a one-time decision. We must decide to obey every day, every time and in every circumstance. Do you know what the Israelites did right after they crossed the Red Sea? They started complaining. They spent a few days in the wilderness and immediately lost sight of what God had done for them.

Obedience starts small

They set up camp and then discovered that the only water in the area was bitter. Then they let panic overtake their hearts. The bitterness of the water went straight to their hearts and poisoned their thinking in an instant. They let their everyday trials overshadow the mighty miracle God had just done for them. I mean, seriously? They just walked right through the middle of a sea on *dry ground*. That had never been done before. It was a miracle of gigantic proportions. Yet after they tasted a little bitter water, everything came crashing down.

But isn't that so easy to do? I have found that it is easier to feel all the good feelings and say all the right things when I'm faced with an impossibility. It's the everyday problems that feel so manageable. I really think I can take care of them myself. Then when I realize I can't, I become just like the Israelites. I'm crying to God, telling Him I can't see Him and my problems are all going to gang up and overwhelm me. We feel like we're going to drown from a teeny sip of bitter water after we already walked through the ocean. *Just like the Israelites.*

When you read what God said to them, you realize it was all just a test. Just like in the "stop game," there was no real danger. God had it under control. He just wanted to see how deep their trust went. And sadly, it wasn't heart deep.

God gave His people test after test, chance after chance. But they never let it penetrate all the way to their hearts. The generation that left Egypt never made it to the Promised Land. They never learned to bow in brokenness to God and say, "Your will be done, LORD." They never learned to take the next step in faith, shielding their hearts from the fiery darts of doubt that the devil kept throwing at them.

The Bible says that their constant disobedience and doubt put them to shame among their enemies (Exodus 32:5). God lays it out very clear in Exodus: if you honor Him with obedience, then He will bless you and carry you on eagle's wings (Exodus 19:3-6). But if you choose to disobey, He is just as able to put you to shame, and you will certainly never reach the Promised Land. Even Moses never entered the Promised Land because of disobedience. This is serious stuff. Obedience is extremely important to God.

When we disobey, we are going right back to the original sin in the Garden of Eden. We consider ourselves to be wiser than God. We are telling Him that He is not big enough to take care of our problems and we are better than Him. Friend, this is pure foolishness. We cannot afford to let this be us. Do not sacrifice your reward to stubborn pride. God has plans for you, and they include doing great things for Him in the Promised Land.

The power of obedience

Obedience is not just an action though. It is a weapon, and it is probably one of the most effective weapons we possess against doubt and backsliding. When we choose to obey God, we are ultimately moving forward, never back. We are keeping our focus in the right place, shielding our minds from the darts of doubt that the enemy hurls at us.

Are you scared of teaching your child God's word? Just take the next step. Does going against the grain of our culture put fear in your heart? Walk forward in obedience. Is God calling you to make a change, but the prospect has left your terrified? Move ahead in simple obedience, and He will straighten the path ahead and open the sea before you. When we walk in faithful obedience, there is nothing we need to fear. Charles Spurgeon puts it this way: "Often depression of spirit and great misery of soul are removed as soon as we quit our idols and bow ourselves in obedience before the living God."[1]

If we are going to teach our children to follow God, we must show them what it looks like to be obedient, no matter what. Every step of our obedience is another stone in the foundation of their faith. Let's build it strong and true!

We can learn so many lessons from Bible stories. The rise and fall of every Bible story hinges on obedience. How did the Israelites conquer Jericho? Through obedience! Why did Samson fall to his enemies? Because he disobeyed God. What brought victory in the lives of David, Daniel, Deborah and King Hezekiah? Strict obedience to the commands and laws of God. The downfalls of Saul, Solomon, Ahab and Jeroboam were because of a complete lack of respect for the statutes of God. They considered themselves wiser than God and so thought His laws foolish.

Isn't that the devil's oldest trick? He made the commands of God look foolish to Eve, took away her respect for the One Who created her and then spoke to her pride. There is not one of us who aren't susceptible to the exact same tactics. But there is good news because our greatest weakness is also our most powerful weapon. When we shield ourselves by absolute obedience to God, the darts of the devil go flying back at him, just like a boomerang, causing great damage in the enemy camp.

When we stand up against the lies of the devil, bravely yelling the battle cry of obedience with all of our hearts, I believe it strikes terror in his heart just as it gives strength to our bones and courage to our souls. Obedience is powerful.

The delight of obedience

There is another side to obedience, a sweet and precious side. Not only is it a powerful weapon important for our well-being, but it is full of delight. The truth is, the Creator of the Universe cares so deeply and personally for *you* that He takes the time to show you exactly the way you should walk. You can trust Him to never lead you astray and to always have your absolute good in mind. The delights of obeying Someone who loves you so intrinsically knows no bounds.

If obedience strikes fear in your heart, remember the example Jesus left for us to follow.

> "Let this mind be in you which was also in Christ Jesus, who, being in the form of God, did not consider it robbery to be equal with God, but made Himself of no reputation, taking the form of a bondservant, and coming in the likeness of men. And being found in appearance as a man, He humbled Himself and became obedient to the point of death, even the death of the cross. Therefore God also has highly exalted Him and given Him the name which is above every name, that at the name of Jesus every knee should bow, of those in heaven, and of those on earth, and of those under the earth, and that every tongue should confess that Jesus Christ is Lord, to the glory of God the Father" (Philippians 2:5-11).

If Jesus knew obedience was so important that He would follow through with death on a cross and endure the separation from His Father, then we can also know it's important above all else. So how do we learn to embrace obedience consistently? Through practice, practice and more practice. This isn't something that is going to happen overnight, so have patience with yourself, and most of all, pray for God to gift you with the spirit of obedience and to fill you with the grace to trust and follow Him.

The Bible says that Jesus "learned obedience by the things which He suffered" (Hebrews 5:8). When you ask God to take you deeper by teaching you obedience, know that it won't be easy, but it will be worth it. Just ask and then take the first step forward. You'll be so glad when you do.

Read Philippians 2 over again. What does it speak to you?

_____
_____
_____
_____

When is a time that you have obeyed God in a hard moment?

_____
_____
_____
_____

Have you been resisting obedience in an area of your life?

_____

What is the first step you can take forward in obedience?

_____
_____
_____
_____

"Blessed is everyone who fears the Lord, who walks in His ways."
—Psalm 128:1

chapter three

Living in Joy

"Joy is not gush. Joy is not mere jolliness.
Joy is perfect acquiescence, acceptance and
rest in God's will, whatever comes."
—Amy Carmichael[1]

He was living in the middle of nowhere. Caves were a luxury, but the open sky and twinkling stars were much more familiar. He spent every day with a sword at his side, keeping the hilt within his grasp throughout the night. He was fierce, courageous and anointed. He could fight a hundred warriors single handedly and was the greatest hero in his nation. Righteous, innocent, loved by God, yet running for his life. He was broken, obedient and *full of joy in his God.*

You see, the people who left Egypt weren't the only children of God who had a wilderness experience. David knew the wilderness very well. It was where he was schooled, and when he graduated, he was destined to be known as one of the greatest men that ever lived. It was the lonely wilderness training that made him the fierce warrior King we all know so well. A man after God's own heart.

David would've been a very interesting person to know. His character assets went deep. He was so broken and transparent that we can still feel his pain today through the Psalms he wrote. He was so obedient that he refused to harm his worst enemy with even a scratch. But it is his joy that I love the most. Even the most broken Psalms have an element of joy and praise that overrides the pain.

The beauty of the wilderness is that we learn to find joy in the driest, most joyless places. Joy is the element that makes all bitter things sweet, just like the branch Moses threw into the bitter stream called Marah, making it drinkable (Exodus15). If only the children of Israel had put their eyes on God, rather than on themselves. What a beautiful lesson of joy they could have learned! Of course, their circumstances weren't lovely at the moment, but if they had chosen to be joyful instead of complaining, the wilderness experience would have been transformed into a thing of rare beauty.

What is joy?

Take a moment to think about joy. What comes to mind when you hear that word? Bubbly happiness during a wonderful occasion? Delight on a perfect day? Or something deeper and more abiding? True joy from God does not depend on any circumstance, neither is it something that can be manufactured by a mere human. Joy comes from a trust that is deeply rooted in the goodness of God. Joy comes from learning to know God through brokenness and follow Him through obedience. It is the natural outcome of a wilderness experience when one's heart is fixed on God instead of on self. Joy comes as a gift from God.

In her book *Hind's Feet on High Places*, Hannah Hurnard chronicles the story of a young girl called Much Afraid. She is taken on a journey to the High Places by the Chief Shepherd Himself but has many lessons to learn on the way. One lesson she learns is the power of choosing to wear the flower "Acceptance with Joy" rather than the "Weed of Impatience." When she accepts the path set before her with joy, it is much harder for her enemies to get the best of her. This is such an important lesson.

Joy is a powerful weapon, able to defend us from darts of bitterness, self-pity and selfishness. While it is a gift of God, there are choices we must make before He pours it out on us: mainly, the lessons learned before — brokenness and obedience. Joy is the road created by the intersection of brokenness and obedience. When we say, *"I will walk where You lead. I will allow You to break me, and I will choose to rejoice in Your goodness,*

God," we are cultivating our hearts to receive the seed of joy that will bloom and grow for as long as we let it.

Joy is a gift, but it is not one that God forces on us. We can choose to give it back at any time.

The joy seed

The seed of joy can come in many different forms, but often it comes masked in loneliness. Initially it feels hard and sharp. It is something from which we want to walk — even RUN — away from. We don't want to embrace the hard feelings of abandonment and aloneness. I have asked God to give me joy and then argued with His method of delivering the gift. I didn't want to deal with hurtful words. I didn't want to walk the long road to the gift of joy because the path of loneliness looks dark, and the thought of walking it alone is so daunting.

As women, we are social creatures. We love to share our thoughts, our journeys, our feelings and more. We feel loved when we can identify with others, and the thought of walking a path alone and unseen often fills our hearts with fear. Who will see our accomplishments? Will anyone notice we've grown? What about when we need a hug? It was these questions that made the road to joy look so terrifying to me.

One of the reasons motherhood is so lonely is that we spend so much of our time unseen. Our moments of deepest growth happen at night when the rest of the world is sleeping. Our choice to obediently follow God goes unnoticed because the only people around are our children.

But loneliness is an important part of the journey. Why did God take the children of Israel out to the wilderness on their way to the Promised Land? So they would be alone. He wanted them to be separated from the distractions around them, so they could learn Him. So they would know they could trust Him and find their joy in Him alone.

We must all go through seasons of loneliness in order to know that we can find our joy in the Lord, to know that He is sufficient for us, right now, in the moment. When we are alone, we learn that Jesus is all we need. We learn that God can perfectly fill the hole left by the lack of recognition and appreciation. When we learn to let Him be our all-in-all, we are suddenly filled with joy. So choosing joy means to deliberately walk into brokenness and move forward in obedience.

But it doesn't end with just choosing joy; the flower of joy must be cultivated. Every December my husband gives me a beautiful poinsettia plant. I love the splash of color and life it adds to my décor, but by January I usually start neglecting it. I may forget to water it for a few days and then that stretches out to a week, and pretty soon it will lose its beauty. The bright and colorful flowers begin to fall off and ultimately disappear altogether. When I neglect the flower of joy, the brightest and best parts will also soon fall away and be gone. Thankfully, there are many ways to cultivate our joy and cause it to flourish.

Go to the Word

The Word of God holds the answer for every question or problem we may have in life. It is infallible, absolute and inspired. When your flower of joy needs to be watered, go to the Bible. Nehemiah 8 tells the story of the Israelites hearing the word of God read aloud in Jerusalem for the first time since their Babylonian captivity. They celebrated with a feast and great rejoicing because they understood the words of the Lord. God's Word is powerful food for the plant of joy. Drink it in and soak it up, because your heart cannot remain joyless when it is infused with God's Word.

Spend time with other Christians

David says in Psalm 122:1 that going to the house of God makes him glad. It fills his heart with joy to be with others in God's presence. Even if you're walking through a lonely stage right now, even if God is doing a work in your heart that is unseen by others, you can still find joy in seeking the presence of God in the company of other believers. Do not let hurts and loneliness keep you away from the rest of His children. There is joy to be found there!

Talk about it

How do we know that David was joy-filled? Because he couldn't stop talking about it. The Psalms are bursting with joy; each Psalm is laced with praise and rejoicing. No matter how lonely, overwhelmed or hurt David was, he chose to proclaim the joy of the Lord.

So when Jesus has filled your heart with joy, let it out! Don't hold it in. Stale joy becomes dead joy. We have to live it out. Even if there's nobody around to share it with, sing out your praise to God. Talk to Him, write to Him, and sing to Him. David had so much joy in following God's commandments that he was out dancing in the streets. God loves to see us living out the joy He gives us. And the results? More joy! It multiplies over and over again until, before we know it, we are overflowing with infectious, life-giving joy. Shout it out!

There are many more ways to cultivate the joy God pours into us. Ask God to show you how to keep your joy not only alive but thriving.

Have you seen loneliness produce joy in your life? How?

_____
_____
_____
_____
_____
_____
_____
_____

Scholars believe David wrote Psalms 7, 27, 31, 34 and 52 while in the wilderness, probably the loneliest time of his life. Choose one to read and write down your impression.

_____

_____

_____

_____

How can you start cultivating joy today?

_____

_____

_____

_____

"In Your presence is fullness of joy; at Your right hand are pleasures
forevermore."
—Psalm 16:11

chapter four

Mistaken Identity

"Therefore if anyone is in Christ,
He is a new creation. The old has passed
Away and all things have become new."
—2 Corinthians 5:17

I stood just outside the plane, waiting for my checked luggage to show up. The man standing beside me was from the same area as our family, and we started chatting about random things. He asked what my husband did for work and then came the inevitable question, "So what do you do?" My answer felt weak, and I could've felt embarrassed. "Oh, I just take care of the kids," I said quickly, trying to judge his reaction.

Seriously? Why does the job title of "Mom" make us feel inferior? Of all of the great callings on earth, God called you to be a mother. And whether you're a stay-at-home mom or a working mom or something in between, your most important job description is "Mom." As Charles Spurgeon put it many years ago: "You are as much serving God in looking after your own children and raising them up in God's fear, and minding the house, and making your household a church for God, as you would be if you were called to lead an army for the Lord of Hosts."[1] Um, *wow*! That is a powerful statement. Obviously we have no reason to feel inferior in our job as a mom.

But we do. We hang on tightly to that insecurity, feeling like out of all the things we should or could be doing, raising our children is the lowliest of callings. We want to do something great that requires boldness and courage. Something that will make people sit up and take notice. So we belittle ourselves and make jokes about how we spend our time, acting as if the greatest thing we do all day is referee our fighting children. But our job is so much bigger than that. It's time to change our perspective, Moms. We need to let go of our self-made identity and ask Jesus to recreate us into the warrior woman He originally intended us to be. And it *will* take courage and bravery, possibly more than we can imagine.

The truth is, our slight embarrassment about being "just a mom" or placing our kids above our "real job" is only a symptom of a bigger issue, deep inside our hearts. We all have wounds and broken places in our souls. I'm not talking about the good brokenness that we talked about in chapter 1, but about holes in our identity, often caused by things that happened while our character and personality were still being formed. These holes are tripping us up and keeping us from living out our calling with boldness and joy.

If you were in a boat full of holes, even tiny ones, you would soon notice that the water seeping in was weighing it down and holding it back from its full potential. And eventually, if left un-mended, even the smallest holes can sink a boat. The same is true of your heart; if there is even one tiny hole that allows water to seep in, your spirit will grow heavier and heavier. So often we focus on bailing the bad stuff out rather than mending the holes. We tell ourselves we are strong, we can cope, we are bigger than the hurts and we have what it takes to "rise above it." But do those words alone fix the holes or do they only stall the inevitable sinking?

"But I don't know how to fix the leaks," we say. "I'm not a shipwright. Building and mending boats is not my thing. Bailing water out is *easy*." It's true that bailing water out of a boat is easier than repairing it, until you get tired. Until you can no longer cope or paste on a brave face. But friends, we know the master Shipwright. And we can take our broken, full-of-holes heart to Jesus, and He can heal our brokenness and make us stronger than we ever imagined.

In other words, we can't just throw off the inferior feelings we are dealing with. We can't mend the holes in our hearts ourselves, and we can't form our own identity into a thing of beauty. But we can step into the mighty power of Jesus Himself and hear Him say "Now you will see what I will do" (Exodus 6:1).

Where to start

Now I want to say, even after all of that, that of course, your calling as a mom is not your identity. Once again, our struggle with being "just a mom" is only a symptom. We often feel embarrassed of our *calling*, but only because we do not embrace our true *identity*. Instead we have stepped into a mistaken identity. Our calling is what we do, but our identity is who we are. Even if our calling got stripped away, even if God took away our job as a wife, a mom or anything else, our identity would still be left. And it is our mistaken identity, wrongly based on what we do instead of on who God says we are, that makes us feel like our calling is weak.

So, what is our identity? Who are you, really? This is what who God says you are:

- Righteous, perfect and blameless
- Loved
- His Daughter
- Called
- A Victorious Overcomer
- A Warrior

And much, much more, but it would take too much time to go over each aspect of our identity as children of God. I love God's description of us because it is big, bold, unexpected and *true*. And maybe even more than I love it, the devil hates it. He does not want us to believe we can be all those things and so he starts chipping away at our identity before we even know we have one. He lays in wait for us and preys on our most vulnerable parts during our most vulnerable times. And soon he can make us believe we are flawed, dirty, unlovable, not good enough, guilty, fatherless, weak and easily defeated.

This list breaks my heart. It is hard to even put into writing. So many of us women believe the devil's description of us much more quickly than we believe what God says about us. And that is the cause of those holes that can eventually sink us, unless we go to the Master and allow Him to make all things new in our hearts.

Friends, we cannot effectively battle for our children when we spend all our time bailing garbage out of our own souls. We must be able not only to focus outwards, on our children, but also to fight for them offensively, before the enemy attacks them. If we are aware of what is going on around us, then we can keep the devil from pounding holes into *their* hearts. But if we are so focused on simply staying afloat ourselves, we won't be completely available to guide our children to the Master when we see lies start seeping into their souls.

We have all given into a mistaken identity somewhere in our lives. Let's take that to Jesus and allow Him to give us a new identity for His glory.

Take some time to pray and search your heart. Ask God to reveal any part that has leaks in it. Write down your thoughts here.

_____
_____
_____
_____
_____
_____
_____
_____
_____

In the next chapter we will start mending these holes with God's truth.

"Through God we will do valiantly, for it is He who shall tread down our enemies."

—Psalm 60:12

chapter five

Mending the Holes

"My faith rests not in what I am, or shall be,
Or feel, or know, but in what Christ is, in what
He has done, and in what He is now doing for me."
—Charles Spurgeon[1]

In the last chapter we talked about the holes the devil has pounded into our hearts from the time we were young. Today we are going to go to the powerful Word of God and refute each lie the devil has thrown at us with God's truth. There is power in being a child of God and it's time to start living it.

We are only going to cover a few main issues many women deal with. I know there are more, so take time to look beyond this discussion and ask God to open up your heart to the holes in your own life. I'm pretty sure each of us have dealt with or are now facing at least one of these identity issues, so this is a great place to start.

Righteous, perfect and blameless

Shame and condemnation have a strong and sticky grip. Once we get caught in their grasp it can feel impossible to get loose. They are bigger and truer to life than the bully on the playground and much more dangerous. Shame whispers our failures to our hearts as condemnation hits us over the head with them like a baseball bat. Only you know the full impact their hold has on your heart. Whether it is the result of the actions of others against you or bad decisions you yourself made, it can be equally damaging. Either way, there is only one effective way to get condemnation off your back: allowing another Person to take it for you.

My dear friend, if Jesus is Lord of your life, then you can let Him defeat that condemnation in your heart forever. The truth is, He already carried it and put it to death for you when He died on the cross. It truly is not your load to carry anymore, and it is time to throw away the deception that says it belongs to you. "Therefore, if anyone is in Christ, he is a new creation; old things have passed away; behold, all things have become new...For He made Him who knew no sin to be sin for us, that we might become the righteousness of God in Him" (2 Corinthians 5:17 & 21). This is the beautiful truth that the devil does his best to hide from us because this truth is *victory*.

And it is the victory of Jesus that rescued us from the darkness of shame and condemnation, for which reason we can say, with Isaiah, "I will greatly rejoice in the Lord, my soul shall be joyful in my God! For He has clothed me with garments of salvation. He has covered me with the robe of righteousness" (Isaiah 61:10). No longer do we need to wear the rags of shame, sin and condemnation! Not only have our spirits been made new through the victory of Jesus, He has literally clothed us in HIS righteousness for the whole world to see. Let us rise up, own those beautiful robes He bought with His precious blood, and walk in the victory that is already won.

Loved

So many women feel they are not loveable or even worthy of love. We believe so many lies related to this stronghold. Some of us may feel bound to earn love by performance; others feel like they can never do enough to earn anyone's love, especially God's. Maybe you feel like you've messed up too many times with your kids and they can never love you now. Those are all lies, I promise you.

The truth is, each of us *have* sinned. We have *all* done terrible things that have wounded Jesus and that others consider unlovable. But that is not what God says He thinks about us; He makes it as clear as can be in His word. "But God demonstrates His own love toward us, in that while we were still sinners, Christ died for us" (Romans 5:8). Friend, Jesus loves you, right now! He loved you yesterday, last year and two decades ago and He will love you forever.

His love is deep, wide, high and completely unfathomable. It goes beyond just love; Jesus *delights* in *you*. He rescued you from your sin, and He exults in that victory. Zephaniah depicts that love in a vivid word picture: "The LORD your God is in your midst, a Mighty One who will save; He will rejoice over you with gladness; He will quiet you by His love; He will exult over you with loud singing" (Zephaniah 3:17).

See, not only does He love you wildly and fiercely, but He wants to comfort your aching, tattered heart with His love. Accept it. Receive it. Drink it deep into your heart. And then, along with David, praise Him for His fathomless, undying love. When you struggle to feel loved, praise Him for loving you anyway. One way to gain victory over this stronghold of feeling unlovable is to actively praise God for loving you in the middle of your most unlovable, messy moments.

"Oh, give thanks to the God of heaven, for His mercy endures forever" (Psalm 136:26).

His daughter

How would you feel if I told you that you were a princess? Maybe like I was being a little childish or fanciful? Then who do you feel like you are in the family of God? Do you sometimes think you aren't quite as good as all the other Christians in your life? Like maybe, if God put all His people in order according to importance, you'd rank as a servant. Never could you fit in with God's elite, the royals of His kingdom.

I do not know why we feel the need to rank ourselves as followers of God, but we do. It's true we are all servants of Christ, but we are more than that. *You* are more than that. All of your life, you may have been told you just do not measure up. You might feel you do not quite fit the mold of who you are supposed to be. Perhaps you feel you belong to God, but on a lower rank.

This is not true. You are as special and delightful to God as if you were His only daughter. He has placed His love on you, and He wants to see you live freely and joyfully in that love.

Now I have to say, I love princess stories. I love all the grandeur, mystery and royalty that makes them what they are. One of my favorites is the story of Cinderella, as told in the movie *Ever After*. But there is one element in the story that always confuses me just a little. Why did she not own who she was? She lived as a servant and masqueraded as a courtier, but the truth is she *was* the daughter of a courtier, and she just allowed herself to be made a servant.

Don't we do the same? We are scared to claim the title of "King's Daughter" for a number of different reasons. We may feel like it would look presumptuous, or we fear we will get written off as fanciful and overly-romantic. We don't want others to think we're living in a dreamland or trying to come across as extra spiritual; we are afraid to claim our identity as daughters of the most High God.

Can we stop and think about this a little bit? How did we become daughters of the King? Certainly not through our own nobility. Not because of all the great things we've done or because we've achieved some great milestone in Christianity. Not even because we were born as princesses. No, there was a time when each of us was living like a ragged street beggar, stooping so low as to sling mud at the Son of the King. But thankfully, that's not where our story ended. Because that very Man we mocked through our pride and arrogance came back when we had nowhere else to turn, and He bought us back to Himself at the cost of

His own blood. And then, instead of condemning us to a life of slavery, which He had every right to do, He *adopted us into His family.*

"'But now,' thus says the LORD, your Creator, He who formed you, 'Do not fear, for I have redeemed you; I have called you by name; you are Mine" (Isaiah 43:1)! How can we shrink away from accepting the new identity He has given us, as His beloved daughters? To not accept the title of the King's daughter is a direct slap to the face of the One Who died to save us. Oh friend, let's not allow ourselves to be deceived into false humility. True humility is to accept the gift offered and live in such a way as to bring honor to the One Who freely gave it. "You shall be called a new name, which the mouth of the Lord will name. You shall also be a crown of glory in the hand of the Lord, and a royal diadem in the hand of your God" (Isaiah 62:2-3). He has given you a new title and a new identity. It is a gift of love. Live it freely and walk royally in the love that comes with it!

Called

Do you ever feel like you just kind of fell into the job of parenting? Like sure, you'll accept the responsibility of children since God gave them to you, but that's not what your real calling in life is. Just like Scuffy the Tugboat, you think in your heart, *"I was meant for bigger things than this."* Maybe being a mom is a dream come true for you, like it was for me. Still, I never thought of it as a calling in itself until I actually found myself in the middle of it. I thought I would have to wait out the years of raising children, making plans for how I would move mountains for God when I was free to do so.

Well guess what? Not only are we free to start moving mountains right now, that is precisely what we are supposed to be doing. Do you think for a moment God was surprised that you are parenting right now? Do you think He created your child and then said "Oops! I guess I'll have to send her on a detour. She'll have to take the scenic route until she can send this kid out into the world and get busy for Me again." Um, no.

But we secretly think that sometimes, and it's an outright lie from the devil about one of the most important callings we will receive in our entire lives. God spoke to Jeremiah directly about the call He placed on his life. And He speaks the same thing to us. He made plans for you too, before you even existed. And this is what He's saying to each one of His children: "Before I formed you in the womb, I knew you; before you were born I sanctified you" (Jeremiah 1:5).

Maybe you recognize the holiness of your calling as a mom. Maybe it feels too big for you. Maybe you can't believe that you are worthy to complete the task of raising children for Jesus. This is just as big of a boat-sinking leak as belittling the call of motherhood. God tells us He will equip those whom He has called rather than call those who are most fit for the job. Just run through almost any Bible story in your mind, and you'll know exactly what I mean. However, God doesn't just demonstrate His desire to work through the weak, He plainly tells us that it is what He's planning. "[God] has saved us and called us with a holy calling, not according to our works, but according to His own purpose and grace which was given to us in Christ Jesus before time began" (2 Timothy 1:9).

When doubts and fear threaten to make you cower at the size of your calling or you feel tempted to minimize what God has asked you to do, pray this verse and claim victory in Jesus. It is yours. "The Lord will perfect that which concerns me; Your mercy, O Lord, endures forever; do not forsake the works of Your hands" (Psalm 138:8).

Victorious overcomer

Another lie the devil loves to bog down our souls with is that we are weak and cannot live in victory. Once again, like he does with every other lie that keeps us from our full potential, he has probably been working this one into your heart for years. It may have started from verbal abuse, bullying, low self-esteem or other things. But the main point is that **it's a lie.** When I started looking into what the Bible has to say about us

38

being overcomers, I got the message loud and clear: We can live in victory! We are overcomers! There is nothing weak or defeated about the Christians who are daily living out God's calling on their lives with grace, faith and trust. Here are just a few examples of scriptures about victory:

"These things I have spoken to you, so that in Me you may have peace. In the world you have tribulation, but take courage; *I have overcome the world*" (John 16:33 – emphasis mine).

"Yet in all these things we are more than conquerors through Him who loved us" (Romans 8:37).

"You are of God, little children, and have overcome them, because He who is in you is greater than he who is in the world" (1 John 4:4).

"Who is he who overcomes the world, but he who believes that Jesus is the Son of God" (1 John 5:5).

Warrior

God created you to be a warrior woman with a fearless heart fixed on God. Every single truth we talked about in this chapter is wrapped up in one word. "Warrior." The Merriam-Webster dictionary describes it as "a person engaged or experienced in warfare."[2]

Whether you like it or not, you are engaged in warfare. We are in the middle of a battle for our very souls and for those of our children. And like it or not, there is no neutral ground. We are either for God or against Him. The line was drawn in the sand long ago, and our only choice is which side we're on. Charles Spurgeon reminds us, "If you are idle in Christ's work, you are active in the devil's."[3]

This is not a truth that our enemy wants us to grasp. He wants us to be mediocre, unaware of the battle, and uninterested in our identity as warriors. If he can keep us distracted and fill our hearts with holes caused by busyness, unworthiness, shame or other lies, he is much closer to winning a victory in our lives or in the lives of our children. Remember, he wants us to be focused inward, bailing out the water, keeping ourselves afloat, so that we are incapable of fighting for the vulnerable and innocent around us.

So what does God's Word say about us being warriors? A whole lot. In fact, God speaks about the battle we're in all throughout the Bible. Every story in Scripture, even the Old Testament, has a two-fold purpose. They all serve to teach us some aspect of God's character and to tell the beautiful story of His romance with mankind. But they also have hidden meanings, spiritual lessons tucked into the tangible, everyday lives of people who are forever woven into the history of this world. These lessons are especially easy to find in David's story. Even his Psalms are rich with allegories and spiritual metaphors. David wrote a Psalm of praise, summarizing his life, and if one Psalm was written for warriors, this is it. I'm going to highlight a few verses here, but please take the time to study it yourself. It is rich with purpose and training for the warrior heart.

> "God is my strength and power, and He makes my way perfect...He teaches my hands to make war, so that my arms can bend a bow of bronze. You also have given me the shield of Your salvation; Your gentleness has made me great. For You have armed me with strength for the battle; You have subdued under me those who rose against me" (2 Samuel 22:33, 35, 36 & 40).

We may not always feel like warriors. We are weak, easily distracted and so human. But this is the beautiful thing about God's kingdom; He calls us to Himself, gives us our mission and then trains us in it as we go. There is no reason to wait for perfection before acting. He will teach us as we go, and the more we practice stepping into our true identity, the stronger He will make us. He will make us great through His gentle instruction and give us the strength we need for each battle we face. And soon we won't just be fighting the battles brought against us, but we will be running out to meet the enemy with swords drawn, defending and defeating through the very power of God!

Bringing it all together

In summary, if we're going to be effective in the battle, we must claim our identity in Christ. Take time to prayerfully identify those holes in your heart that are threatening to sink or incapacitate you. Search the Scriptures and find verses to refute each lie the devil is throwing at you to keep you down. Dig deep into the hurts and wounds you've received. Open your heart to God and allow Him to probe with His sometimes painful, but always healing touch.

Do not be ashamed of the scars from old wounds. Each scar serves a purpose and will most likely never be completely erased.

To put this on a physical level, my Dad has a very large scar across his torso, a reminder of the time that his skill saw got caught in his shirt and ripped his chest open, narrowly missing his heart. But that wound has healed now, and the scar only serves to remind us of how God spared his life. Soul wounds can be healed in the same way if they are taken to the Great Physician and given over to His care. Clean them with honest searching, put the salve of truth over them and wrap them in heartfelt prayer. Then stand back and allow God to have His way. He will pronounce you righteous, loved, royal, called, and victorious, a Warrior in His mighty army.

Yesterday you identified some holes in your life that were holding you back. Go back to those and search the Bible to find what God says about those areas in your life. (A simple search in the Bible app or with your favorite search engine will work well for this.)

Write down the references that spoke to your heart:

41

_____

_____

Now write those verses down on index cards and place them around your house where you can read and pray them every day.

Be intentional about claiming your identity through Jesus, every day.

"For though we live in the world, we do not wage war as the world does. The weapons we fight with are not the weapons of the world. On the contrary, they have divine power to demolish strongholds. We demolish arguments and every pretension that sets itself up against the knowledge of God, and we take captive every thought to make it obedient to Christ."
—2 Corinthians 10:3-5 NIV

Part 2: What She Does

"For You have armed me with strength for the battle;
You have subdued under me those who rose against me."
—2 Samuel 22:40

chapter six

Why We Fight

"Everything finds completion in Him."
—Colossians 1:17

In 1772 a young man named Timothy Thayer enlisted in the Continental Army. When he failed to meet up with his company at the appointed time, the commander started asking around. It didn't take long to discover that Timothy Thayer was actually a woman named Deborah Sampson. She was, of course, not allowed to join and voluntarily returned the bonus money she had received.

Not to be easily defeated, Deborah took it a step further and, because of her height, was able to join the Light Infantry Unit in another town. This elite unit was comprised of larger and stronger men, and so there was less of a chance she would be suspected and caught again. This time her plan worked.

Deborah was wounded in the first skirmish she took part in, taking two musket balls to her leg. Her fellow soldiers threw her on a horse against her will and took her to the army hospital. Determined not to be discovered, she snuck out of the hospital and pulled one musket ball out with a penknife and sewing needle, but was unable to get the second one out. She continued to fight after that though her leg never fully healed.

What would cause a woman to keep fighting so tenaciously, even though she was wounded and had to go through more hardship than the average soldier for the sake of keeping her gender hidden? The explanation is simple: *she believed in what and who she was fighting for.*

How about you? What is it that's putting fire in your heart? What is awakening your warrior heart and compelling you to fight? Is it your children? Memories of your own childhood? A desire to look good to those around you or fit in with other moms in your church? Maybe you're passionate for your child to serve God, to go further than you, or maybe you have a whole host of reasons. Maybe it's just because "that's what you do."

While many of those reasons are good ones, there should be more to it than that. If we fight just for our children's sake or to fit in or feel like a good Mom, we will fall short and end up feeling defeated and disillusioned, our fire dwindling to a glimmer rather than a red hot flame.

Could there really be a more noble reason to fight for our children's souls beyond simply fighting for them because they're our children and we love them? Here's what Paul says about it: "And whatever you do in word or deed, do all in the name of the Lord Jesus, giving thanks to God the Father through Him." (Colossians 3:17).

If everything we do is to be centered on Jesus and done in His name, then the only conclusion we can draw is that everything we do, including raising and fighting for Godly children, is done for Jesus first of all. Isaiah also talks about how we were created for the glory of God: "Everyone who is called by My name, *whom I have created for My glory;* I have formed him, yes, I have made him" (Isaiah 43:7 – emphasis mine). This means everything we do should be done for His glory first, and then all the other good reasons will fall into their proper places.

Why it matters

So why the big emphasis on raising our children for God's glory above anything else? I mean, fighting to raise Godly kids is good and noble, right? Yes, of course. And you may be successful if that is your end goal. But if we all shift our focus just a bit, if we would all aim a little higher,

46

just think of the strong message we would send to the enemy camp and, more importantly, to the heavens themselves.

When I was a teenager, there was a lofty quote floating around that basically said "Shoot for the heavens; if you fall short, at least you'll land among the stars." I never really liked it. Why couldn't I just aim high and hit high? If the heavens was the goal, why not work to hit it rather than simply sigh and be happy for how far I did get?

God has big plans for you, friend. And beyond that, He has big intentions for you. He intends for you to shoot farther than you can ever imagine possible, not for yourself, but for His glory. He isn't interested in how you look to others as much as He is in how you fight for Him. He wants to be your sole focus and your only goal. He wants you to do more than dream big or plan big – He wants you to fight big. And so He gives you His own mantle of strength to do it with. God has not set us up for failure; He has set us up for victory. He does not just place big desires in our hearts, but He equips us to reach them, *with His help*.

And so it is only natural that all of our fighting and pressing forward is done for Him, first and foremost. If someone gave you a valuable gift to complete an enormous project or mission with, would you continue working for your own satisfaction or shift your goal to make your benefactor proud for the trust he placed in you? God has given each of us a gift of immeasurable value, and He intends for us to use it to shake the very foundations of hell. The best reason to do it? *For His glory!*

"As it is written, 'He who glories, let him glory in the Lord'" (1 Corinthians 1:31).

There's more

So we have this amazing gift from God: the power to fight in His strength and win the victory. But that's not all He's offering us when we give the battle to Him. There are so many benefits to fighting for God's glory first, above anything else. Because in the end, we can fight and pray and do everything we can to raise our children to serve Jesus, but there will most likely be some disappointments along the way.

Our children may not see eye to eye with us, they may hurt us or we may be misunderstood by others as we raise and fight for the little ones in our care. But when we're fighting for God above all else, He is the shield that will take the hit for us.

In 2 Samuel 22, David says "The Lord is my rock and my fortress and my deliverer; the God of my strength, in whom I will trust; My shield and the horn of my salvation, my stronghold and my refuge; My Savior, You save me from violence" (verses 2&3).

When doubts come driving into our hearts and Satan whispers that we have failed, we can take it to God. If we have been grounded and focused on Jesus before anything else, we have no reason to carry the weight of condemnation around. We can know that nothing we have done is a failure because we have done it for the glory and love of Jesus. And love never fails. Jesus never fails; He is ever faithful. Though our work be tested with fire, He is faithful.

And we can know this: our work *will* be tested with fire. Satan is not going to sit passively by, letting us win the victory. He will test everything we do, and what's more, God will let him because fire refines, and in the end, the fire will shout out the glory of the Lord. Because everything that is built to the Lord will be built with things that cannot burn, so that when it passes through the fire *it will stand,* to the glory of God.

In the moments when everything seems to fall apart, we can rest in God. We can know that He still has it all under His control and that the victory does not rest on us but on *Him.* He has already defeated death, sin and the devil. He has already won the victory, so if we are battling for Him, the victory is won. He has not surrendered His authority and He never will.

Weak things made strong

On our own, we are not warriors. By ourselves, we are weak and powerless, lacking the wisdom and know-how it takes to win a war. This is exactly how God created us, and He designed us that way for a reason. He does not intend for us to fight on our own. In fact, it is His design that we know our weakness so we can step back in awe at what He does through us.

When Paul was writing his first letter to the believers in Corinth, he let them know just how weak he was when he was with them. He told them He did not come with perfect speech or wisdom, preaching the gospel of Jesus. He was determined they would not come away remembering *his* awesomeness, but only the glory of Jesus, crucified, risen and standing in as a ransom for our sins.

Paul knew that his words, his passion and his fighting alone were not enough to bring people to Jesus and win a victory. It was only Jesus, working beyond Paul's weakness, who would win. It was Paul's very weakness that put Jesus in the spotlight, and so it should be for us (1 Corinthians 1&2). Truly, the weaker you feel, the greater things God can do through you. Our human weakness is not something to fight against; it's a gift from God to keep us humble and, ultimately to allow Him to show His power and win the victory.

Making it practical

There are a lot of voices out there boldly proclaiming that we are warriors, we are brave and we should do hard things. We are so often told how wonderful we are that we forget we are nothing on our own, and we owe it all to Jesus. And we forget that with all the brave and true words we hear, there must be an actual application in our lives.

How do we go about raising our children for Jesus first of all? It starts in the heart, then the mind and then shows through our actions. I'll probably live it out differently than you will, but that is not the point. The point is to put action to our passion and make it real in our lives.

We can start on our knees, asking God to fill our heart with a deep desire for His glory above our own. We can ask Him to keep us humble and aware of our shortcomings and failures. As He fills our hearts with Himself, our minds will start to wake up and look for ways to put hands and feet to that desire to glorify Him. And ultimately, we will spend more time on our knees, begging God to make it practical to us and then follow in strict obedience.

It won't be easy or glamorous, and it won't necessarily shine bright for all to see. But that doesn't matter when our hearts are fixed on Jesus. Raising our children for the glory of Jesus may look a lot like putting our selfishness aside (Think cell phones and social media). It is going to require each of us to stop worrying what others think of our parenting and possibly to make choices that aren't popular. Because when we are raising children with Jesus as the goal, everyone's feelings will be second to obedience to the Word of God and His gentle leading.

It will take passion, discipline, courage and a deep-rooted love for our cause, namely Jesus. And if we can rise up and do it, despite our feelings and the lack of popularity, if we can put away the romanticized picture of working for Jesus and forget about the fancy words and simply live it out in every day shoe leather, we can know for sure we will reap what we sow. Jesus, only Jesus!

So mama, fight. Fight with courage and passion. Fight for your children's hearts because you love them. They are precious gifts from God. But set your aim a little higher than that and focus on the glory of God. His glory trumps all other reasons, and it is our safe spot as warriors and protectors of our children.

Are there areas in your parenting that you haven't surrendered to Jesus?

_____

_____

Is there anything holding you back from surrendering those areas and fighting for the glory of God first and foremost?

_____

_____

_____

_____

Take some time to pray about practical ways God wants you to raise your children for His glory. Then come back and write down your thoughts here.

_____

_____

_____

_____

_____

_____

_____

"I will praise You, O Lord my God, with all my heart, and I will glorify Your name forevermore."
—Psalm 86:12

chapter seven

Entering the Battlefield

"Finally, be strong in the Lord and in
the power of His might."
—Ephesians 6:10

The young woman threw her arms against the rock behind her and could almost feel it tremble. She lifted her left hand to shield her eyes from the sun, trying to get a better view of the small band of soldiers coming across the plain. Her right hand grasped her sword a little tighter and she reached down to pick up her shield. She paused, gazing at the round disk, her mind leaving the scene around her for a moment.

"But my Lord, these weapons look almost like a child's playthings," she had said hesitantly when she first saw her sword and shield. The King had looked at the young woman and smiled before answering, "There is one lesson you have yet to learn before you can achieve a victory. *You* will never be victorious on your own. And yet you can win every battle if you choose. But each victory must be won through the power of *My* might, not yours. That must be your battle cry in every encounter with the evil forces."

The memory brought a brief smile to the young woman's face as she prepared for yet another battle. It seemed as if she had been fighting one battle after another with barely a break. She smiled again as she got a firm grip on her shield. The King had not told her that with every battle won her weapons would become stronger instead of worn down— the blade of her double edged sword seemed to grow sharper after each victory. The shield was now a massive piece of armor that had saved her life on more than one occasion, and she continued to grow in skill with both weapons.

She glanced up. Three formidable-looking men in full armor were closing in around her. The large rock behind her protected her back, and she was thankful for it. She checked her breastplate and braced herself for another battle. She had been tired and discouraged a few moments before. Now the memory of the lesson her Master had taught her gave her new life. Her eyes shone with hope and determination as she readied herself to fight for the King and her children.

"I claim victory for the King! I fight you in the power of His might!" Holding her sword in front of her, the King's warrior quickly shattered the silence. Her attackers paused almost imperceptibly and then continued toward her silently. Next to break the silence came loud clashes of sword against sword and sword against shield.

"You are all alone, fool. The King is far away and His power cannot help you here. You are in *our* power." The large soldier in front of her smirked and attempted a thrust into her chest.

"The King's power never leaves those who fight for Him — our very weapons are filled with His might!" The young woman quickly deflected his blade and once again shouted "the power of His might!"

The battle was long and hard. Moving slowly from the east side of the meadow, the sun seemed to pause overhead and then began to slip down toward the west. The evil of the three large soldiers was almost tangible and seemed to thicken the air. The soldier to the young woman's right dropped back in a sudden change of strategy. She glanced at him momentarily and wondered if he was retreating from the battle.

The man grinned viciously and began a verbal attack, making it hard for the champion of truth to concentrate on the battle. "The King has filled your weapons with the power of His own might? Do you really believe that? It's all lies — lies He uses to bring people into His pitiful little Kingdom. Have you ever seen any part of the Kingdom He professes to reign over? He has tricked you, and now you will die because of your stupidity."

He paused, and another malicious grin ran across his face as the young woman seemed to falter for a moment. His grin quickly turned to a disappointed scowl as he saw the King's warrior once again deflect a blade wielded by one of the soldiers of darkness. He had clearly hoped it would be the death blow.

The evil soldier continued his bantering toward the young woman, never pausing for an answer. The soldier to the left seemed to grow tired and the young woman started directing her efforts towards him. Immediately the soldier that had been talking jumped back into the fight, allowing his tired partner a brief respite. Now the second soldier took up the mocking of the King and His soldiers.

This pattern continued into the evening as the sun turned from its scorching yellow to a blaze of orange and began to sink behind the trees in the distant horizon. The young woman was at the point of exhaustion and didn't know how she could continue any longer. She had never fought so hard and long in her life, and these were most formidable foes. Her shield was getting too heavy for her, and she was getting slower with her sword. To give up was unthinkable, and yet was there another option? The fact that she was fighting two soldiers instead of three did not make it any easier because the constant mocking confused her mind.

The third warrior chuckled as he watched the young woman struggling for her life. "She's not so sure of herself now, is she? This he directed to his two companions, and they grinned as they continued to battle. "Look at her," the evil opponent continued, "She's not fighting for victory anymore. She's just trying to stay alive."

His eyes glittered and he laughed. "You aren't going to win this victory, are you? You with your special kingly weapons. Those were just dreams, weak one. Nobody has ever been victorious over us. What makes you think you would be any different? The King's got no special interest in you. He never gave you His power." He chuckled again, deep, dark and evil.

But the large soldier made a mistake with his last statement. "The King's power!" the young woman thought. "This isn't my battle. It's the King's!" She felt new hope coursing through her veins. Her enemies expressions quickly turned from cruel arrogance to dismay as the young woman once again shouted her battle cry.

"By the power of *His* might!!"

They screamed curses at her, but she heeded them no longer as she continued to yell her battle cry. She fought with such a burst of strength that it was over before the sun could completely disappear.

She slowly put her sword back in its scabbard and let the shield lean against the rock. Once again she saw someone walking toward her across the plain. This time she ran to kneel at the feet of her King.

"Through the power of Your might," she said softly. The King reached down and pulled her to her feet, holding her close in a fatherly embrace. "You have learned the lesson well, and so the victory was won. For no matter how alone you may feel, I am always close beside you, and you will always be victorious when you are strong through Me and trust in the power of My might."

Not many mighty are called

Mama, on our own we are nothing. We are not warriors because of our own goodness or skill. We do not win battles against the devil because we are great. Nothing we do will prosper unless it is held up by God's mighty strength. Without Jesus, we have no hope in the battle. The sooner we understand this, the sooner we will become victorious.

It sounds like a contradiction to embrace the fact that we are weak and helpless so we can win spiritual battles, but this is the beauty of how God works. Paul explained it this way to the Corinthians: "For you see your calling, brethern, that not many wise according to the flesh, not many mighty, not many noble, are called. But God has chosen the foolish things of the world to put to shame the wise, and God has chosen the weak things of the world to put to shame the things that which are mighty...that no flesh should glory in His presence" (1 Corinthians 1:26, 27 & 29).

God delights to choose the weak, unimportant, and sometimes even the despised things of this world to do His work. In this way, our pride must always take the back seat because we know victory is impossible for us to achieve by ourselves. God gains glory through every victory because it is obvious that we cannot win through our own strength.

Humanly speaking, in the story above it was absolutely impossible for one young warrior to make it through the fight against three seasoned soldiers without losing her life, never mind defeating each one. Yet God loves to show Himself strong in impossible situations like this. He purposely chooses those of us who are weak, incompetent and unschooled to do His work and fight in His battles, so that our fighting actually becomes a form of worship as we yield ourselves to His power working through us.

A couple of weeks ago I found myself in a slump. I was so exhausted I wasn't sure if I could keep going another day. Coffee did not give me even a five minute boost. Our entire family had been sick for weeks and the lack of sleep was making life miserable. When I finally realized that the devil was filling my heart with discouragement I was able to give my lack of energy to God. And the energy that He infused into my body was wonderful. The energy He gave my heart was even more amazing. I was able to walk in victory and even be an encouragement to those around me instead of dragging the entire household down. God is faithful and His strength is perfect for our weaknesses.

When we realize and accept our complete weakness without God, He can take us to new heights in our walk with Him, and we will find ourselves going from victory to victory. As Oswald Chambers puts it,

"Complete weakness and dependence will always be the occasion for the Spirit of God to manifest His power."[1]

Making it practical

Did you know that even the apostle Paul taught the gospel in "fear and much trembling" (1 Corinthians 2:3)? When I think of him, I imagine a man with fire in his soul that came out through his words. I imagine someone confident, wise and full of power. But this is not how he describes himself. After telling the Corinthians how God uses weak things for His glory, Paul gets a little more personal and tells a story of his own.

> "And I, brothers, when I came to you, did not come with excellence of speech or of wisdom declaring to you the testimony of God. For I determined not to know anything among you except Jesus Christ and Him crucified. I was with you in weakness, in fear, and in much trembling. And my speech and my preaching were not with persuasive words of human wisdom, but in demonstration of the Spirit and of power, that your faith should not be in the wisdom of men but in the power of God" (1 Corinthians 2:1-5).

It can be scary to teach our kids the gospel. Sometimes it feels like walking a tightrope between paralyzing fear and overwhelming pride in our own knowledge. It truly takes the Holy Spirit's leading to do it in a way that glorifies God. The enemy will attack us any way he can. He knows the ones he can't catch in his net of fear will be more susceptible to self-sufficiency and pride. He doesn't care which side we fall on as long as we're falling. This is the first battle we must learn to fight through God's might.

Friend, God wants to use you in a mighty way in the lives of your children. You are called to wage spiritual warfare for them with bravery and persistence. But first you need the victory over whatever might be keeping you from fighting with God's strength. It's time to confess our crippling fear or haughty pride and ask God to fill us with His power. Then we need to come up with a battle plan, put it into action and fight through it with God at our side. When we win that inner victory, we will be ready to fight on the offensive, jumping into the battle before it has even begun.

God is searching the earth, wanting to show Himself strong on the behalf of someone whose heart is loyal to Him (2 Chronicles 16:9). Will you let it be you?

Have you allowed fear or pride to keep you from teaching your children the gospel?

_____

What is the best way for you to combat this obstacle? Ask God to give you a battle plan and write it down here:

_____
_____
_____
_____
_____
_____
_____
_____
_____

"Cheer up now, you faint-hearted warrior. Not only has Christ travelled this road, but He has defeated your enemies."
—Charles Spurgeon[2]

chapter eight

Putting on Truth

"Stand therefore, having girded your
waist with truth."
—Ephesians 6:14

"I am so worn out," I told my husband one evening after he got home from work. I felt close to tears. "I feel like everything I do is a battle. I am fighting for friendships. I am fighting to keep my house neat, fighting to spend time with God and fighting to train the kids. *Everything is a battle.* Can't I have a break already?"

It was a hard season for me. My heart was in constant turmoil, and I found it hard to focus on simply raising our kids with joy. I was irritable, easily offended and completely exhausted. And I felt like I was caught on a treadmill, fighting the same battles over and over without any new results. I knew I was supposed to be living in victory, but I could not for the life of me figure out how.

And then suddenly, one day it clicked. I quieted my tender feelings long enough to listen to God, and He rocked my world. All the battles that overwhelmed me and threatened to send me into despair were of my own making. I was fighting on battlefields that were useless and centered on myself. In my pride and puffed-up knowledge, I had started my own war when I was supposed to be fighting God's battles.

Just like the Israelites in the wilderness, I was going around and around in circles, focused on how I felt, where I was and what everyone might be thinking of me. When God showed me His truth, the path became clear and straight before me. Thank God for His sweet and generous patience towards us. Thank Him for faithfully revealing the devil's deceptions to us.

Foundations

The entire gospel is built on truth. If there is no truth in what we believe, then we are "of all men the most pitiable" (1 Corinthians 15:19). Everything we do, everything we believe and everything we live is girded up in the truth of God's existence, the sacrifice of Jesus and His glorious resurrection. We could not be who we are if it were not for the truth of those things.

Truth goes even deeper, filling up all the little parts of our faith. In fact, truth must permeate every area of our lives, our faith and our parenting if we are to be successful warriors. Truth carries power. It sanctifies and sets us free (John 17:17 and John 8:32). It holds our entire suit of armor together. If there is no truth, then what good are righteousness, the gospel of peace, faith, salvation, prayer or even the Word of God? If there is no truth, then we have nothing. We are nothing.

When we believe and cling to the absoluteness of the gospel we are given the ability to fight through God's might. All of our weapons and protective gear function and stay in place because of the belt of truth we wrap around ourselves. So buckle it on tight because it's the only way you'll live in victory!

Useless battlefields

The devil is out to destroy you. This doesn't sound nice, and it isn't. The truth is he's hunting you like a lion stalks its prey. Always cunning, he knows the best way to keep you from the battles that matter. And here's a tip: he doesn't always lead you completely away from the truth, but he can also distract you with something that *feels* right. As women, we like to be led by our feelings because they're a safe and familiar ground for us. Our feelings are something we know and understand, and it doesn't take much effort or energy to be led by them. Kind of like running on autopilot.

And so we easily fall victim to useless battles of the mind. We analyze friendships, comparing what we have with what others have. We give into feelings of hurt and exclusion, believing others would rather not have us around. And you know, sometimes the hurts are real, but we need to look at the truth and disregard our feelings to divide right from wrong correctly.

The truth is, friendships can be hard. We do get hurt, and our feelings get bent out of shape. But we need to realize those hurts are hardly ever meant to be the battle—they are just the training. God allows hard things to happen to us so that we can be strengthened into better warriors and shaped more into His image. But when we turn our strength to fight against God's training rather than against our real enemy, we have given into deception. Our costly distraction allows the enemy to buy up the valuable ground of our children's hearts while we are focused on other things.

Another distraction the devil loves to throw at us is our children's behavior. We quickly allow ourselves to be reduced to referees fielding arguments, or we get so wrapped up in their childish feelings that we become slaves to them when we should be their guardians. We become so focused on the here and now that we forget to train their hearts for the future, spending our time bandaging their feelings instead. For example, when my child is hurt by another child I can choose to focus on their feelings or gently teach them how to forgive. The first choice is only a Band-Aid while the second one is equipping them to be warriors in the future.

Sometimes it's sheer exhaustion that gets us to throw in the towel for a while because *Mommy just needs a rest*! The struggle is real, folks, I know! But if the devil can get us distracted from the truth until we've worked ourselves into an exhausted state, then he has won that round. When our focus shifts to our exhaustion and immediate circumstances, we forget the importance of the battle we've been commissioned to fight. But when we stay focused on the truth, we are able to receive the strength and grace we desperately need.

There are a lot of other useless battlefields the devil uses to distract us with, and they are each uniquely tailored to us. The point is, he will use those deceptive battles to get us worked up into such a frenzy and self-centered state of exhaustion that that we can no longer fight effectively on the frontlines. We are no longer capable to protect our children from his attacks. If we quit being guided by truth and become easy prey ourselves, our ability to protect our children from Satan's attacks weakens. When we forget to walk in line with the truth, we are one step away from becoming a casualty of war.

Fighting the lie

So how do we battle these distractions and keep our spiritual power? Through the grace of God and a holy pursuit of the truth. If we passionately seek truth, God will show it to us. If we are willing to obediently walk away from the useless battlefields we are tempted by, God will be delighted to open up a path for us in the wilderness if need be.

In order to step away from a useless battlefield, we need to discern truth from lies. Satan hardly ever feeds us a whole lie; he often mixes truth with it. It's like he gives us a counterfeit belt for our armor: the leather may be sound, but the buckle that keeps it in place is plastic and will never hold up.

Let's take the case of a difficult friendship, for example. The truth is that a hard relationship can come with a lot of pain and secret hurts. The lie is that we need to focus on those hurts. What we need to do is take each hurt before God and ask Him to show us the lesson He wants us to learn. When we have done that, we can simply believe that He has us in that situation for a reason and choose to move on with our life as He leads.

Charles Spurgeon shared a powerful truth we can use to deal with a hard situation, "Remember this: had any other condition been better for you than the one in which you are, divine Love would have put you there."[1]

This doesn't mean the hard part will immediately disappear, but it will give us the freedom to move on to fight the battles God has called us to rather than floundering around in a no man's land of our own feelings. If we love God, then we will love and rejoice in the truth even when we don't love the circumstances (1 Corinthians 13)!

Becoming a lover of truth

Truth isn't always comfortable. Sometimes it would feel good to let it slip a little and just relax, like loosening your belt after a Thanksgiving dinner. But we are warriors, and we cannot afford to let truth slip because, if it does, our entire suit of armor will go with it. We have to learn to embrace truth and hold it close even when it gets uncomfortable, and our kids need to see us do this on a daily basis.

On the whole, our society does not love truth. Many people do not want to deal with the discomfort it brings. A lot of us Christians don't really love the truth either. It feels so much easier to let a few of the more difficult Bible principles slide. We want to fit in with our friends, and we certainly don't want to look strange to anyone. We would hate to stand out. And so we fit ourselves right into bondage, because a lack of truth is bondage.

Out of kindness to us, God set up truth as a boundary. When we live in His truth, we are safe from deception and secure in His presence. But when we start living outside of truth, we will quickly be overtaken with confusion, and everything will become blurred and gray. We will no longer be capable warriors infused with God's strength; instead we will find ourselves wandering around like the blind leading the blind.

To protect ourselves from that fate, we need hearts that fiercely love the truth and will not be tossed and turned by every false doctrine that blows our way. Our hearts have most likely been damaged by the storms of doubt and human reasoning that blow against God's holy truth. We need them to be pure and sanctified again so that we can rightly discern and lead our children in the truth. Thankfully the Bible tells us exactly where to go for that sanctification.

As Jesus was praying for His disciples, just hours before He was arrested, He said these words, "Sanctify them by Your truth. Your word is truth" (John 17:17). Jesus showed us exactly where we need to go and what we need to do in order to become lovers of the truth.

First, we need to pray for it; second, we need to go to the Word of God and immerse ourselves in it. If we fill ourselves with truth, we will naturally come to embrace and love it, until finally it becomes a vital part of ourselves.

Immersing yourself in truth will look different for you than it does for me. We can go after the truth in so many different ways. It is important to map out a battle plan that works for you and then stick to it! Here are a few different ways to get you started:

- Write verses down on index cards and post them all over your house and even in your vehicle.
- Listen to an Audio Bible while doing things that don't require much mental energy, such as washing dishes, folding laundry or cleaning the floor.
- Start your morning out with God's Word before anything else. Go straight to the Source of truth.
- Have an action plan ready for those times your mind wants to wander to the distractions, i.e., start praying for someone, praising God or reciting Scripture.
- Find someone who will keep you accountable and help you stay on track.

Creating a battle plan and sticking to it will strengthen all of your spiritual muscles, and you will find yourself equipped to fight the battles you face with more strength and power than you realized was possible. Remember this: truth always wins the war. Let's choose the winning side!

Have you been fighting on a useless battlefield? What is it?

_____

_____

What truth can you apply to the situation?

_____

_____

_____

Map out a battle plan to combat the enemy in this area of your life. Write it down and put it somewhere you will see it often.

_____

_____

_____

_____

_____

_____

"All the paths of the Lord are mercy and truth, to such as keep His covenant and His testimonies."
—Psalm 25:10

chapter nine

Wearing Righteousness with Grace

"Put on the breastplate of righteousness."
—Ephesians 6:14

Whenhen God created man, He created him to have an open relationship with Himself. We were created to have a friendship with our Creator. This always amazes me. God is perfect and complete within Himself and has no need for any other being. But *knowing* that mankind would turn their backs on Him, *knowing* it would take His Son's death on the cross and *knowing* all the rebellion and heartache that was to come, He still wanted our companionship.

And so He created us in His own image and placed within us an ever-living soul. This soul is the very heart of us, and it is precious to God. He underscores its importance over and over again in Scripture.

Because of this, the hearts of my children are extremely important to me. The entire reason we as moms fight for our children is to win their hearts. The very essence of who they are, their hearts are the part of them that will live on forever, in an eternity filled up with Jesus or completely void of Him.

And so we fight for their hearts. We pray for them and take time to nurture and care for them, doing our best to pour in good things that will cause them to grow strong and true. We cultivate their hearts to beat for Jesus and His Kingdom.

I am a "mean" mom. My kids haven't watched the latest movies, and they aren't allowed to play with our phones. We went on a 5,000 mile road trip last year, and the kids watched a total of three movies. You might be a mean mom in different areas. No matter what areas we decide to be strict in, we know the importance of screening our kid's activities, especially when they're young. We consider the influence of the people they hang out with and take time to pray for them. We teach them Bible stories and verses, take them to church and send them to Sunday School, all in an effort to care for and nurture their hearts.

But in all of our care, if we do not show them how to *protect* their hearts, our work will never last. I can keep my kids from anything I consider a bad influence until they're grown up, but if I don't also use that time to teach them the "why" behind the decisions and the value of caring for their own hearts, then I am missing the most important part. The heart needs to be protected and encased with a piece of armor so thick that the enemy's darts cannot pierce it through.

God has given us the breastplate of righteousness just for this. He could've chosen anything, but in His perfect wisdom He knew righteousness would be the best for the job. We cannot force our children to wear this breastplate as they grow up and make their own choices, but we *can* show them what it looks like to wear righteousness with grace and strength, while also protecting our own hearts and motives.

There are two things we need to do to effectively put on the breastplate of righteousness. First, we must realize our righteousness is nothing apart from Jesus. Our own righteousness is like filthy rags in His sight and just about as protective. As we already briefly covered earlier, we are sanctified and perfect in the sight of Jesus. He has covered us with His own cloak of righteousness, and He sees our hearts as perfect.

All we need to do to have a righteous heart is allow Jesus to renew it with His own blood.

The attack

The devil hates our righteousness. He hates that Jesus has made our hearts blameless in God's sight. He would love nothing more than to soil our most vital part with his nastiness. So he comes at our hearts over and over again. He forms weapons that aim at our weaknesses. One of his main goals is to obliterate our righteousness, so he will do whatever he can to cause us to stumble and fall into sin.

He knows that if we fall once, we become more susceptible to his darts and will fall easier the next time. The devil is cunning and patient. He will chip away at your righteousness for years, and he is in no hurry when he feels like he's winning.

The thing with the devil's darts is that they don't often look dangerous. They look nice, and we actually *want* them. He appeals to our flesh, the most human part of ourselves. In our hearts we are as perfect as if we were already in Heaven with Jesus, but the earthly part of us is still susceptible to the sin of the world.

Paul talks about this paradox in Galatians, saying "So I say, walk by the Spirit, and you will not gratify the desires of the flesh. For the flesh desires what is contrary to the Spirit, and the Spirit what is contrary to the flesh. They are in conflict with each other, so that you are not to do whatever you want" (Galatians 5:16-17).

Can you relate? I sure can! I know what is right. I know how I should treat my husband, my family and my friends. I know how to live rightly. But then a dart of selfishness gets thrown at my chest, and it actually feels good! I *want* to live in my feelings. I want to cut out friendships that aren't going great, and I want to care about my own comfort before my husband's. I want to zone out with my own projects rather than spend time with the kids. Not always, of course, but the desires are there. And sometimes they're really strong!

So how to protect our hearts from these vicious but well-disguised attacks?

Putting on righteousness

It comes down to choice. We can chose to put on the breastplate of righteousness or go to battle without it. We can choose to protect our hearts in humility or proudly consider ourselves unsusceptible. To wear the breastplate of righteousness is to choose to live rightly in the face of discomfort, fleshly desires and even laziness.

Sometimes this is harder than it sounds. In the highest moments of our quiet time, after a church service or during time spent with godly friends, we glibly imagine ourselves as warriors of righteousness, skillfully wielding our swords and offsetting the enemy's attacks. But in the loud moments of parenting, the days filled with sickness, disobedience or drama, the choice to live right appears foggy and unclear. Should I discipline the child I can hear being mean or linger in the presence of Jesus just a little bit longer? Should I spend the afternoon with a friend who needs someone to talk to for a few hours or finish that project my husband would love to have done?

Yet righteousness does not come before truth. There is a reason Scripture tells us to put on the belt of truth *before* the breastplate of righteousness. Truth is our guide and the key to living righteously. When we learn to measure our everyday decisions against the truth of God's Word, we will learn to live righteously. God actually has a lot to say about how we should live, and it's time to sit up and listen!

Paul gives a lot of hints in Galatians. The first key?

Love.

Practical righteousness

"You, my brothers and sisters, were called to be free. But do not use your freedom to indulge the flesh; rather, serve one another humbly in love. For the entire law is fulfilled in keeping this one command: "Love your neighbor as yourself" (Galatians 5:13-14 NIV).

"The fruit of the Spirit is love, joy, peace, forbearance, kindness, goodness, faithfulness, gentleness and self-control. Against such things there is no law" (Galatians 5:22-23 NIV).

To put on righteousness is to put on love. Our breastplate is fashioned out of the precious metal of love. When we put our love for others above the selfish love of ourselves, we will live righteously without even trying! What does this look like? Something like this:

Practical righteousness is being quick to hear, slow to speak and slow to anger (James 1:19). It is kind, tenderhearted and as forgiving as Jesus (Ephesians 4:32). Living righteously means to put anger, wrath, malice, slander and dirty talk far from us (Colossians 3:8). It means to walk in a way that is worthy of our calling as children of God, embracing humility, gentleness, patiently bearing with each other in love and being eager to maintain the unity of the Spirit, peacefully bonded together with other children of God (Ephesians 4:1-3).

Our children need to see us living out this kind of righteousness in our relationships. They need to feel it being applied to themselves and observe it being freely given to everyone who crosses our path. They need to see it at home and when we're out and about.

My five-year-old recently learned to wash the dishes, and she loves doing it. I am always a little nervous because cups and plates break easily in our sink. A little while ago she broke one of my favorite juice glasses while trying to organize the dirty dishes to wash. She felt so bad and was getting teary-eyed. Instead of reacting in a negative way, which was tempting, I gave her a hug and helped her clean up the mess. I'm not telling this story to highlight my own righteousness because, trust me, I'm not perfect. But what impacted me from this small event is that she remembers my reaction as positive and is starting to connect the dots: this is how *she* should react too when someone ruins something of *hers*. No act of righteousness is too small; our kids don't miss a single one.

Daily righteousness

I would love to give you a chart, with everything neatly mapped out, to show you exactly how to make those hard decisions and how to choose to live rightly every time, but I can't. God has given us clear guidelines to living righteously, as we just saw. However, we cannot make these daily little decisions and choices between two "rights" by working our way through a chart, but we can learn to make them in a God-honoring way by seeking the heart of God.

Our hearts were created to live in perfect communion with Him, and the only logical way to learn to live rightly is to know His heart. God tells us "You will seek Me and find Me when you seek Me with all your heart" (Jeremiah 29:13 NIV). And He has given us this promise: "I will give you a new heart and put a new spirit in you; I will remove from you your heart of stone and give you a heart of flesh. And I will put my Spirit in you and move you to follow my decrees and be careful to keep my laws" (Ezekiel 36:26-27 NIV).

As believers, we have received a gift from God — He has put a little part of Himself into our hearts. But so often His voice gets drowned by the noise and chaos of everyday life. In the busyness of dishes, laundry and even teaching little hearts, we forget to be still and listen to God's guidance. But listen to this: *He cares* about our everyday moments. He knows when we are worn out and it's hard to focus, and He wants us to come to Him. He wants to guide us on the path we should take. All we need to do is let Him.

When it comes to choosing rightly, we must use the Bible as our absolute truth and then rely on God to show us. We can see, by the Pharisees' example throughout the gospels, that living by a list of rules only leads to more rules and a completely different path than what God intended.

Seek the heart of God, give your daily moments to Him, and He will guide you in the right choices and decisions. Don't wait for the big moments to choose the right thing. Let's remember the power of starting small. If I cannot make the right choice between folding the laundry or catering to my own selfish whims, I will not be ready to choose the right way when it comes to difficult parenting, marriage problems or moral living. We must start small; no small, but right decision has ever been wasted, and this will always hold true in our lives.

Graceful righteousness

All of this righteousness talk can start sounding a little "holier-than-thou"ish. Living right so we can rub it in our children's faces when they mess up isn't going to do us any good. Seriously, when I think of righteous living, I think of the Pharisees. They had so much right. While it may seem like being "perfect" came naturally for them, we should remember they were human too. Their biggest god may have been the fear of man, but it surely wasn't their only weakness. They worked hard to be righteous, yet they still fell short because they made righteousness their sole aim and their god.

We cannot wear a breastplate of righteousness forged out of love while walking around with a self-righteous air. True and graceful righteousness is the natural outflowing of a heart that is fixed on and in love with Jesus. A heart that recognizes it cannot live righteously on its own.

A friend of mine came over for coffee one day, and we sat talking over some difficult issues. She poured out her heart, and I listened — and then offered my own un-asked for "wisdom." She kindly told me she wasn't really looking for answers; she just wanted to talk. I still blush at my hasty self-righteousness. My words had not stemmed out of love for my friend, but from a haughty love of my self-made wisdom. This is not graceful righteousness. It is really nothing but pride and imagined importance.

Friends, we don't have the power to live rightly on our own, and when we throw our wisdom around like confetti on everyone who happens to sit beside us, *we are failing*. When we allow pride to seep into our hearts until we turn our noses up at everyone who doesn't meet our own standards, *we are failing.* We are failing miserably. There is no place in God's army for someone who takes glory for themselves. We are nothing without Jesus, and our goodness is nothing apart from Him (Psalm 16:2).

Our heart cry should echo that of the Psalmist: "My flesh and my heart may fail, but God is the strength of my heart and my portion forever" (Psalm 73:26 NIV). We are human, and we may fail. But God…God is our strength and our portion; He is our life, forever. We cannot be righteous without Him.

Righteousness is not weak. The breastplate is one of the strongest parts of our armor, created to take direct hits from a powerful weapon and withstand the force. Choosing to do the right thing is never a weak decision, no matter how it may look to those watching. Our King is a mighty warrior, and nothing He does or calls us to do comes from weakness, no matter how it looks. Every piece of armor He has given and everything He commissions us to do is born of His might.

Put on your breastplate boldly and wear it in sweet humility before your King, protecting the precious heart He has given you.

What does righteous living mean to you?

_____

_____

_____

_____

_____

_____

Spend some time asking God to show you how you can apply the breastplate of righteousness to your everyday life in a practical way. Write down any verses or thoughts here.

_____

_____

_____

_____

_____

_____

_____

_____

_____

_____

_____

"Above all else, guard your heart, for everything you do flows from it."
—Proverbs 4:23 NIV

chapter ten

Moving Forward in Peace

"And having shod your feet with the
Preparation of the gospel of peace."
—Ephesians 6:15

T he soldier carefully buckled her belt, followed by her breastplate
and helmet. She polished her sword and checked the soundness
of her shield. Piece by piece, she readied her weapons for battle.
When she was confident everything was ready, she sat, waiting for the
battle to come.

That's never how the story goes, is it?

It is sad to see a talented person who never tries to reach her potential.
We are each created to fill a purpose for God on this earth, and it is our
sacred duty to do it. It is as silly for us to sit around waiting for our
purpose to fall in our lap as it is for a soldier to get ready for battle and
then sit in her room.

If you are a mom, then you have an important job to do. It is our
purpose, during this season of life, to raise our children in a way that is
honoring to the Lord. It is our job to protect our children before they
are attacked, not reactively as each battle comes. If we as moms sit
around waiting for the battle to come to us, there will be no victory. By
their very nature, the shoes of the gospel of peace are telling us to "get
moving," and they're not talking about the gym.

No land was ever conquered by an army that stayed home. And no peace
will be gained by sitting around in our armor waiting for war. What does

it mean to march in the shoes of the gospel of peace? Surely it means to actively share the good news of Jesus!

When I hear the word "peace," I think of a calm quietness. I picture everything in its place while I relax with all my work done. I like to think of quietly reading to my kids while soft music plays in the background. Nobody is loud, and nobody is fighting. Flowing from my own peaceful attitude, a calmness reigns.

And then I think, "Ha! That will never happen." And I give up on peace during this season of life.

However, there is a difference between the English word "peace" and the Hebrew word "shalom," and it is worth looking into. When the Bible talks about peace, of course it uses the Hebrew word, which is more powerful and carries several different meanings. "Shalom" has been translated as "peace," but in translation it loses some of its power. Shalom conveys the idea of being complete or sound. It speaks of safety in mind, body and estate. Biblical peace is powerful and perfectly fits in with the rest of our armor.

The valor of a peaceful heart

> "The peace of God, which surpasses all understanding, will guard your hearts and minds through Christ Jesus" (Philippians 4:7).

Peace is not just some weak feeling. It is a bodyguard especially designed to protect our hearts. A peaceful person has courage like no one else. When we allow the inner peace of God to wash over our hearts, an inner strength comes with it. No longer are fearful or tumultuous thoughts allowed to have the upper hand. They are put on the run by peace!

A personal battle of mine has been fear. Sometimes I used to lay awake for hours at night, too fearful of the bad things that might happen if I fell asleep. This fear hindered my parenting, mostly because I was often so exhausted from lack of sleep I could hardly function. I needed peace to take over my mind and give me rest.

As moms we really need peace. So many thoughts and circumstances can threaten to take over our minds until we are living in a state of turmoil. We all know that raising kids is not for the faint of heart, but some days we give into faintness anyway because motherhood is a job so much bigger than we are.

We need a plan of action to keep peace alive and well in our hearts. And as always, God already has that plan ready and waiting for us in His Word.

> "Be anxious for nothing, but in everything by prayer and supplication, with thanksgiving, let your requests be made known to God and the peace of God, which surpasses all understanding, will guard your hearts and minds through Christ Jesus" (Philippians 4:6-7 NKJV).

> "You will keep him in perfect peace, whose mind is stayed on You, because he trusts in You" (Isaiah 26:3).

We need to look at peace as an action verb. It is not a passive feeling, but rather a conscious choice followed by deliberate action. When anxiety and worry threaten to overwhelm us, we need to take our fears to God along with our praise. When we do, He promises that peace will guard us. It steps in like a body guard whose job is to fight off all our anxious thoughts and worried feelings.

When our outward circumstances overwhelm us, we can anchor our minds on Jesus. When we actively focus our minds on Him, He keeps us with His perfect peace. It *is* possible to focus on Jesus rather than an unknown future. It *is* possible to look to Jesus rather than being fearful of the opinion of those who are watching us. We can deliberately choose to focus on Jesus no matter what our outer circumstances may look like. We are always safe when our minds are fixed on Jesus above all else.

Righteousness and peace have kissed

"Mercy and truth have met together; righteousness and peace have kissed. Truth shall spring out of the earth, and righteousness shall look down from Heaven" (Psalm 85:10-11).

"The fruit of that righteousness will be peace; its effect will be quietness and confidence forever" (Isaiah 32:17 NIV).

God created His armor to work together. No piece is independent from the others and no part can replace another. Working hand in hand with righteousness, peace guards our hearts and minds when we focus on the truth of the Bible. We cannot have a peaceful heart if we are not living righteously, just as a soldier loses her effectiveness if she fails to put on either her shoes or breastplate. We cannot know how to live righteously if we are not founded on the truth, just as the belt holds the breastplate in place.

Going to battle for God and our children is all or nothing. Either we put on all the armor or we go into battle unprotected.

The gospel of peace

Peace is not selfish. When we put on the shoes of peace, we are getting ready to go somewhere. These are not soft house slippers intended for our own comfort. These are shoes created for walking in treacherous places, the kind of places you wouldn't want to go barefoot. Places only those armored with the shoes of the gospel of peace would think of going. These shoes were created for a war waged to bring peace and safety to mankind, and we get to be part of it.

Soldiers rarely enter a war for their own purposes. They fight for their commander and believe in his reason for fighting, and they fight for the love of their country.

We as Christians also do not fight for our own purposes. We fight for Jesus and what is dear to His heart: the souls of men, women and children. We fight so others can have a future in Heaven, our eternal country. When Jesus was on the earth, He left a clear example of what it looks like to wear the shoes of the gospel of peace. He sought out the lost, the outcasts and the downtrodden, and when He found them He *served* them.

The shoes the Romans soldiers wore were made with metal spikes on the bottom. They made a loud noise when the army was marching, they helped the soldiers keep their footing and they were used to trample the enemy under them as they advanced. Our shoes of peace have spikes as well. However, we don't put on our shoes to trample people underneath us. We put them on so we can stand our ground against the enemy. And then we use them to spread the gospel of Christ wherever God has called us to serve.

Wearing the shoes God gives us means stepping out of our own comfort zone and showing up for those who need peace and comfort in their lives. It means living with a mindset of service that puts others ahead of our own comfort. When we put on the shoes of the gospel of peace, we are committing to show up.

During the time I was struggling so heavily with fear, God was calling me to minister to other moms. He put a message on my heart, but I ignored it, and I asked God, *"Who am I, anyway? I am not experienced like other moms. My children are still young, and I don't have the answers."* And I reminded Him, *"Fear is kind of beating me up over here. Haven't You noticed? I'm not good enough to encourage others."*

But when I finally gave in and followed His call, He took care of the details. It turns out I don't have to have it all figured out. I never will and neither does anybody else who works for Jesus. I simply have to point to Him, over and over again. And when I finally put on those shoes of peace and started doing something for God? The fear almost completely disappeared. My mind is now guarded with the perfect, powerful peace of Jesus. Just typing this makes me want to shout "Hallelujah!"

Practical peace

Showing up is going to look different for each of us and it's going to look different during the changing seasons of our lives. Moms with small children may be able to invite the lonely and overlooked into their home for a time of encouragement. They may be able to volunteer at a local mission one day a month. Or they may be living out on the mission field, but don't compare the shoes God gave you to those He gave your sister.

As our kids get older, it will be easier to find ways to serve outside of our homes. However, the temptation may be strong to finally get in a little "me time" after years of attending to every need just to keep the babies and toddlers alive. Strap those shoes on, and don't give in to the temptation! Our children need to see us using them as they are meant to be used. One of the most important parts of being a warrior mom is to be an example to our children. Teaching them is wonderful and necessary, but showing them how to live is even better.

How have you envisioned peace in your home?

_____

_____

_____

_____

What does peace mean to you now?

_____

_____

_____

_____

Spend some time in prayer asking God to show you His vision of the gospel of peace for you. Write it down here. Take time to make it practical (Planning babysitters, making invites, etc.).

_____

_____

_____

_____

_____

_____

_____

_____

_____

_____

"Great peace have those who love Your law, and nothing causes them to stumble."
—Psalm 119:165

chapter eleven

Defending with Faith

"Above all, taking the shield of faith with
Which you will be able to quench all the
Fiery darts of the wicked one."
—Ephesians 6:16

The small army boldly moved their camp into the valley. They were in plain view of the large, walled city. This move was a clear challenge: they wanted war. They were ready to fight, and they were making it obvious.

The King of the city understood the challenge instantly. He must have chuckled to himself. He had easily defeated this army a short time before. Why would they come back for seconds? They were much too small to gain any victory against his fortified city. Eagerly he called his large army together, and they set out against the smaller army that seemed to them more of a sport than a threat.

When the small army saw them coming, they began to run away! The King's army followed in hot pursuit; they were already exulting in their obvious victory. Suddenly the leader of the smaller army stopped and turned. He stretched his spear out towards the city behind them. The large army turned back out of curiosity, and what they saw must have filled them with despair. Their walled city, the fortress they were supposed to be defending, was filled with flames.

Once again God's people defeated a seemingly unconquerable city. While the small army was busy leading God's enemies out of their stronghold, a larger army had been hiding in ambush behind. The Israelites had acted in faith, carefully following the instructions God had given Joshua. While the smaller band may have felt some embarrassment as they pretended to run, they boldly moved in faith. They could've been paralyzed in fear and turned to fight rather than trusting God's plan. Anything but strict obedience to God's instructions would have resulted in defeat and ruin.

They knew this from experience. Dozens of their men had lost their lives only a little while before when they tried to conquer the city of Ai through their own strength (Joshua 7 & 8). Their faith did not always come easily. It was tested, and sometimes it failed altogether. God's people made mistakes, and they paid for them. But rather than leaving His people and going on to search for a more faithful group, God used their mistakes as stepping stones. He turned their failures into lessons and then trusted them with great missions, right after grave mistakes. And so their faith grew.

Where does faith come from?

What is faith? Where does it come from? Is it a spiritual gift? Is it something we grow on our own? How can we live a life of faith if we don't even know where to get it or how to live it? It seems as if some people, such as George Mueller or Amy Carmichael, were just born with it. It seems as if they effortlessly trusted God to carry them. They seemed to instinctively know which way to go and what to do. They stand as shining examples in the faith "Hall of Fame" along with Abraham, Sarah, Joseph, Moses, David and many others.

And here we sit, cleaning up milk spills and washing dishes. The trash is overflowing, and the dishes need to be washed. We feel overwhelmed and insignificant. Why do we need a shield of faith anyway? But the desire to live a life of adventure and purpose for God calls, and we long for our faith to get tested in some big way. We long to prove ourselves as women of faith.

There are times I feel like I would welcome a painful experience so my faith could stretch its wings and soar to the Heavens. But how? And where? I think back to the time we waited for days in a small motel room, waiting to know if the baby daughter we already loved so fiercely and hoped to adopt would be our own or if someone else would get to snuggle her and take her home. But even in the midst of the turmoil, we had a peace and even a certain joy. God was stretching our faith! It was painful, but it *was good*. And while I wouldn't want to live that over again, it also whetted my appetite for more stretching experiences. To live in bold faith is to feel alive!

When the Bible talks about faith, there are several different meanings. First, faith gives us understanding, and it grows by believing in God Himself. Hebrews 11 starts out like this, "Now faith is the substance of things hoped for, the evidence of things not seen. For by it the elders obtained a good testimony. By faith we understand that the worlds were framed by the word of God, so that the things which are seen were not made of things which are visible" (Hebrews 11:1-3).

We cannot be followers and warriors for God if we do not believe in Him. The very basis of our Christianity rests on faith. We believe. We believe God created the world by spoken word. We believe Jesus has come in the flesh to redeem us. We believe in eternity with Him even though we cannot see it.

This is the first step all believers must take. Then it's time to put some action to our faith, as demonstrated by the rest of Hebrews 11. How do we do this?

The answer lies in our everyday life. While we gaze at the mountains of faith we long to have, God is giving us chances to quietly live a life of faith for Him every day, but we shrink away in shock. Hannah Hurnard demonstrates this well in her book *Hind's Feet in High Places*. Much Afraid, the heroine of the book, is on a journey to the High Places with her beloved Shepherd. She longs to live way up on the mountaintops, victorious over her crippling fear and selfishness. The High Places are her destination, and the Shepherd desires to take her to the safety of their heights. But then before she's barely started, the path takes a detour, and she is horrified.

In desperation she calls to the Shepherd, and He affirms that yes, this is the path. It seems to Much Afraid as if her dreams are all melting before her.

> "Much Afraid sank on her knees at his feet, almost overwhelmed. Then he answered very quietly, 'Much Afraid, do you love me enough to accept the postponement and apparent contradiction of the promise, and to go down there with me into the desert?"
>
> She was still crouching at His feet, sobbing as if her heart would break, but now she looked up through her tears, caught His hand in hers, and said, trembling, 'I do love you, you know that I love you. Oh forgive me because I can't help my tears. I will go down with you into the wilderness, right away from the promise, if you really wish it. Even if you cannot tell me why it has to be, I will go with you, for you know I do love you, and *you have the right to choose for me anything that you please.*"[1]

Much Afraid did eventually make it to the High Places. Not because of her own strength or wisdom but because she made deliberate choices to trust each step and detour of the way.

Faith is in our everyday choices. Faith is saying, *"God, you know I love You, and as my God, You have the right to choose for me. You choose my path and I will walk it."*

Faith, like brokenness, is often exercised beside loneliness and sorrow. It looks so glamorous in the stories we read, but faith seldom *feels* glamorous in the moment. To live a life of faith, we have to erase our fairytale pictures and allow God to fill in the lines as He sees fit.

Cultivating faith

Faith is like a seed that God gave us when we gave our life to Him. It was a gift, but now it is our responsibility to cultivate it. Jesus says that if we have faith like a mustard seed, we can move mountains (Luke 17:6). A mustard seed starts out so small, but it can soon grow into one of the biggest herbs, big enough that birds use it as a place of rest!

We can chose to live our day-to-day life in survival mode, leaving no room to step out in faith, or we can chose to live a life of expectation, waiting to see what God might have in store for us next. We can ask God to take us on a journey and then follow His path for us rather than trying to dictate the way from the passenger seat.

God has plans for you, Mama. And chances are they don't look anything like you might imagine. Don't expect big, mountain-moving plans right away. While that may happen to some, it is not the usual way for most of us. Allow your faith to grow in the little areas of your life. We can live a life of faith in the little moments if we have our eyes open to recognize those moments as invitations to faith.

A mighty shield

The shield is obviously a vital part of our armor. Paul places a great emphasis on it, stating "above all, taking the shield of faith" (Ephesians 6:16). The shield was very important to Roman soldiers. There were times a dagger was more important than a sword, or archery was chosen over hand-to-hand combat, but the shield was never optional.

The shield the foot soldiers used was a massive, concaved rectangular piece of wood, metal and leather. It provided vital protection, and the Romans would not have conquered the world without it. It could be used to deflect sword blows in hand-to-hand combat or stop arrows shot from a walled city. When necessary the soldiers would stand closely together to create the "tortoise formation." The front line of soldiers would hold their shields in front of themselves, and the soldiers behind would hold the shields above them, creating a wall of shields that protected from attack on all sides and even above.

Some enemies would literally shoot fiery darts. Historians believe the Romans would dip their shields in water and so quench the fire before it caused any damage. The Romans knew they couldn't go to battle without their shields and the same is true for us as Christians and warrior moms. We cannot be victorious against the enemy if we are not armed and protected by faith. God has given faith to us as a shield. It protects us from the worst darts the enemy has to throw at us. We need to practice engaging it.

When we pray over our children in faith, we are putting them into the hands of God rather than holding them tightly to ourselves. When we choose to believe God can use us in the season we are in, we are living in faith. *Doubt doesn't have a chance in the face of faith.*

 When we believe God has our days planned out and holds us in His hand, we are living in faith. When we trust an unknown future to an all-knowing God, we are living in faith. *Fear shatters against faith.*

When we see hurts as a chance to grow rather than wallow in self-pity, we are living in faith. When we stop asking "Why?" and start looking for the lesson in the pain, we are living in faith. *Self-pity runs from faith.*

When we choose to live our lives for the sake of Christ rather than for ourselves, we are living in faith. When we step away from being known and seek to know God instead, we are living in faith. *Selfishness is quenched by faith.*

New mercies

Faith is possible for every child of God, no matter their circumstances or season of life. We as moms do not need to wait for our children to grow up to valiantly step into the battle with our shield of faith. Neither do we need to hide in our homes, afraid to exercise faith because we have failed in the past. Faith is an ongoing lesson. The Israelites failed over and over again, even after incredible victories. They saw God's power manifested in such real and physical ways it would seem there was no room left for doubt. And yet they stumbled at God's leading right after witnessing His power. But God still used them for His purposes.

It is the same for us. We are human, and we will fail! Our faith will not be perfected after one trial run. We find forgiveness and grace freely given in the throne room of Heaven. "Let us therefore come boldly to the throne of grace, that we may obtain mercy and find grace to help in time of need" (Hebrews 4:16).

Hebrews contains the great "Hall of Faith." It is full of descriptions of men and women who lived lives of faith. They were not perfect people, and the Bible holds the stories of their failures as well as their faith. But they all had something in common: they embraced the promises of God and knew they would come true. "[They] confessed they were strangers and pilgrims on the earth. For those who say such things declare plainly that they seek a homeland. And truly if they had called to mind that country from which they had come out, they would have had opportunity to return. But now they desire a better, that is, a heavenly country. *Therefore God is not ashamed to be called their God*, for He has prepared a city for them" (Hebrews 11:13b-16 – emphasis mine).

They failed, yet God was not ashamed to claim them as His children because they stayed faithful to His promises even after failure.

You may not have lived a life of faith yesterday. You may have made wrong decisions or found yourself paralyzed by fear. Yesterday may not have been a day of faith, but today can be! Jeremiah reminds us of God's faithfulness in the middle of hard times. "This I recall to mind, therefore I have hope. Through the Lord's mercies we are not consumed, because His compassions fail not. They are new every morning; great is Your faithfulness" (Lamentations 3:22-23).

I have seen this verse in action over and over. Just yesterday I gave in to fear as I wrote this book. I was tempted to put it away until I felt like a

93

more accomplished Christian. I doubted God's will in my life even though He has made it clear many times. But today His mercies are as fresh as the snow that came during the night and now stretches as far as we can see, and I am able to continue walking the path He has chosen for me. Our faith may tremble and fail, but God's faithfulness never wavers. And faith is faith when it moves forward after the heart of God, trembling though it may be.

Let us take up our shields and start quenching those darts! God has a mission for each of us and faith is required to complete it.

What is one thing God has been calling you to do in faith?

_____

_____

_____

What is the first step you can take in answering His call?

_____

_____

_____

Find a Bible verse that speaks faith to you. Write it down, put it where you can see it and pray it daily.

"Therefore we also, since we are surrounded by so great a cloud of witnesses, let us lay aside every weight, and the sin which so easily ensnares us, and let us run with endurance the race that is set before us, looking unto Jesus, the Author and Finisher of our faith."
—Hebrews 12:1-2

chapter twelve

Living Salvation

"And take the helmet of salvation."
—Ephesians 6:17a

Before I was married, I worked on a volunteer ambulance service. I lived in a remote rural area, and it would easily take 45 minutes for an ambulance to get back to our community. So when I wasn't at work in town, I was on call as a first responder in the local area. While not many emergencies happened back there, my friends would get me to pull out deep splinters, take care of nose bleeds that wouldn't stop or bandage wounds that made them queasy.

One time I even superglued a gash right above someone's eyelid caused by running into a clothesline. It doesn't take a very big blow to the head to leave a person wounded or disoriented, and every medical worker knows that head wounds should always be taken seriously. This carries over to our spiritual life as well.

"Take the helmet of salvation," Paul says. What does this mean? If we're putting on God's armor, aren't we already saved? Haven't we already put on salvation? Yes, and the men who put their helmets on were already soldiers trained in warfare. They still needed to protect themselves from attacks against themselves and their country. Our souls are redeemed and headed to Heaven with Jesus, but there is still work to be done!

The helmet was designed to take the brunt of any blow to the head. Its job was to protect the brain, which is the command center of the entire body. A heavy blow to the head can damage a person's ability to make good decisions. Nobody can survive the battlefield when their decision making is impaired. Battle requires making decisions in the blink of an eye, and they better be good ones or we're in serious trouble.

Our spiritual helmet carries the same job. In an earlier chapter of Ephesians, before he teaches on the armor of God, Paul says this, "But you have not so learned Christ, if indeed you have heard Him and have been taught by Him, as the truth is in Jesus: that you put off, concerning your former conduct, the old man which grows corrupt according to the deceitful lusts, and be renewed in the spirit of your mind, and that you put on the new man which was created according to God, in true righteousness and holiness" (Ephesians 4:20-24).

When we were saved, a transformation took place inside us. Jesus cleansed our hearts and clothed us with His own righteousness. He made us new and repaired that perfect relationship with Him that was broken in the Garden of Eden. But we are still faced with daily choices, and we do not live in a perfect world yet. We still deal with temptations and have to distinguish deceit from truth. Our minds need to be renewed continually.

The devil loves to sneak up behind us and hit us on the back of the head with a crafty deception. *We need protection.* Salvation is a daily process, not unlike sanctification. Yes, the inside work has been done! Jesus has delivered us from sin; now we need to live that salvation on the outside.

Paul wrote a letter to the Christians in Rome and exhorted them to, "not be conformed to this world, but be transformed by the renewing of your mind, that you may prove what is that good and acceptable and perfect will of God" (Romans 12:2).

We put on the helmet of salvation to protect our minds. Our hearts can be full of so many good intentions, but if we don't keep our minds protected from deception and other blows of the enemy, our intentions will not carry us through. And moms, we can't afford to dream of raising our children for Jesus and not follow through with deliberate action! We are teaching eternal souls, and we need to be fit and clothed for battle in our hearts and minds.

As moms, we tend to fall into two different distractions: pride or busy overwhelm. I find myself susceptible to both, sometimes switching back and forth in just one day! In the morning, I spend time teaching my children from the Bible and pray heartfelt, powerful prayers over them. I leave the couch feeling accomplished. *I'm such a good warrior mom!* A few minutes later my short night of sleep catches up with me, and I find myself angry over a bowl of spilled cereal. *I'm such a failure! Why do I even try to be a spiritual warrior when I'm busy enough simply trying to keep the tiny humans alive?*

I know I'm not the only one. But the good news is it doesn't have to be this way. We have been given protection from the dizzying blows of pride and overwhelm. The key is to *wear it.* So of course, the question follows: how? Every other part of our armor has some type of tangible action associated with it. It's easy to form a plan and follow through. But our minds literally have a mind of their own. We find them wandering before we even realize they've gone AWOL!

Tangible salvation

"Be renewed in the spirit of your mind," Paul says. This is the key to protecting our mind. It needs to be renewed daily, moment by moment, until it is completely subject to the will of God.

Ethel Barret rewrote John Bunyan's classic book *The Holy War* and renamed it *The War for Mansoul.* The story portrays the battle for each person's mind in a vivid and unforgettable way. The army of the King is in constant battle with enemy forces for control of the city of Mansoul.

Mansoul, of course, represents the soul of a man.

The favorite method of the King's enemy to gain control is to infiltrate the town with his soldiers, who drug and imprison old Lord Conscience and then flatter Lord Will be Will until he is willingly won over to their side. This mission is accomplished all too easily. And over the years this still seems to be the favorite method of the devil to con God's children into living a life outside of God's will.

We allow him to silence our conscience as he tempts our will with things of fake value. We allow ourselves to believe we know better than God what's good for us. We fall prey to the same deception as Eve did so many years ago. We believe God doesn't actually know what's best for us, or at least that there may be an easier way to get to His best than the path He has called us to.

We allow our will to be tossed back and forth like a small fishing boat at the mercy of stormy waves. We go back and forth, wanting to serve Jesus in every moment, but then selfishness steps in and we want to live our own way. We toss around between the two until our souls become seasick with the constant back and forth motion. We need an anchor to securely tie us to God's will.

But so often we don't see this, and we try to forge our own path, following our hearts and dreams rather than God's call. We reason that any desire that pops into our Christian mind must be a calling from God, and we must follow it. But this is not always true! Our minds may be redeemed, but God tells us they also need to be renewed. It *is* possible for us to go wrong in following our dreams. Even good dreams must be subject to God's will.

Growing up, I always wanted to be like Amy Carmichael. I had my sights set on India and children's ministry for years. But that's not what God had in mind for me. If I had followed that dream rather than allowing God to write my story, I would not be serving Him as well as I can serve Him here, nestled in my northwestern home with my family.

This is why we need to put on the helmet of Salvation. It works as a filter, sorting out right from wrong and giving us the ability to make clear, God-honoring decisions without faltering between temptation and truth.

We need to take each thought captive like the Bible tells us to. The first step is often worship. When we spend time worshipping our Savior, we become tied to Him through adoration. If our mind is full of the greatness of our God, how will there be room for the enemy to send his minions to infiltrate our thoughts? The devil hates to hear God praised, and the Bible tells us that God is enthroned in the praises of His people (Psalm 22:3). When we praise God, He is dwelling right in our praises, filling up our minds with His presence! We cannot find better protection from the enemy's deceptive blows than this.

When we go to the Old Testament, we find many verses that link God's salvation with praise.

> "O Lord, I will praise You; though You were angry with me, Your anger is turned away and You comfort me. Behold, God is my salvation, I will trust and not be afraid; 'for YAH, the Lord, is my strength and song; He also has become my salvation.' Therefore with joy you will draw water from the wells of salvation" (Isaiah 12:1-3).

Jesus is our Salvation. We need to put on Jesus. He is our protector, our strength and our song! He gives us joy in our salvation. Isaiah brings this point home once again.

> "We have a strong city; God will appoint salvation for walls and bulwarks. Open the gates, that the righteous nation which keeps truth may enter in. You will keep him in perfect peace, whose mind is stayed on You, because he trust in You" (Isaiah 26:1-3).

These passages are so exciting to me. They were written before God's redemption had come, yet He was so excited about His plan to bring salvation to His people, He just had to share the beauty of it.

God is telling us that His salvation is protective. He talks about living by truth and righteousness and in His perfect peace. The touch of God's salvation is woven all throughout the Bible, from the Old Testament to the New.

To put on salvation is simply to live in close communion with Jesus every single day. Our minds cannot be invaded when they are fixed on Him. Instead, they will be renewed day by day. The more time we spend with Jesus, the more we will want to be like Him. Jesus brings salvation to us daily. His mercies are new every morning, and He has a plan for each day that is far greater than we could ever hope or imagine in our wildest dreams, because His plans are centered on His greatness rather than ours.

Putting on the helmet of salvation means waking up each morning and saying, *"Jesus, show me **Your** way today. Teach me Your truth, not mine. Show me the path **You** have chosen for me to walk today. You are the God of my Salvation and I will wait on Your will all day long"* (Psalm 25:4-5).

We can take our weak, ever-changing will and put it into the hands of God. He can renew it and mold it into His own will until the two are one. Will we still stumble from time to time? Yes, we are human! But we will be on God's journey for us, and His path will always lead us upward, closer and closer to Himself.

Taking this path and putting on Jesus as our salvation will not look normal to the world. We cannot fit in with the world when we are wearing Jesus as a helmet of salvation for our mind. Heavenly wisdom does not make sense to the world. The wisdom of God is a mystery; if it were not, the religious leaders would not have had Jesus crucified. God's plans for His beloved ones is also a mystery. He tells us that no one has seen, heard or even been able to think of all the wonderful things God has prepared for those who love Him. (So much better than our own dreams!)

But God has sent His spirit to reveal these things to us.

And God has told us, through Paul, "But the natural man does not receive the things of the Spirit of God, for they are foolishness to him; nor can he know them, because they are spiritually discerned. But he who is spiritual judges all things, yet he himself is rightly judged by no one. For 'who has known the mind of the Lord that he may instruct

Him?' *But we have the mind of Christ"* (1 Corinthians 2:13-16 – emphasis mine).

We have the mind of Christ. Just think about that for a little bit. What an amazing and glorious gift!

There is no five step method when it comes to putting on Christ as our helmet of salvation. It will look differently for everyone. Moms are busy; it's hard (or impossible) to find hours to spend in the Word. But we can still abide in Jesus the entire day. Our spiritual walk will probably look different now than it did before we had kids, and it will look different again when our kids are grown and on their own. But God never said it has to always look the same.

Today, take what you can get. Listen to worship music that exalts *Jesus,* not feelings. Read a few verses of Scripture and dwell on them all day. Ask Jesus to imprint them in your heart. Pause before acting in anger and ask Jesus to renew your mind. Simply take every part of your day and give it to Jesus. Live in an attitude of worship before Him, and you will find your mind protected.

Yes, we will have to make choices, like forgiveness and trust. But if your mind is in the habit of running to Jesus for the everyday happenings, it will quickly run to Jesus in the hard times of life as well.

Jesus took the blows meant for us when He died on the cross. And He is protecting us from the blows of the enemy today, but we must choose to dwell in Him.

What does wearing the helmet of salvation look like for you?

_____

_____

_____

_____

_____

_____

How can you start consistently choosing God's plans for you over your dreams?

_____

_____

_____

_____

_____

_____

Find a scripture to focus on or pray when you are tempted to make decisions without the helmet God has given us. Write it down and run to it whenever you need to.

_____

_____

_____

_____

_____

_____

_____

"My mouth shall tell of Your righteousness and Your salvation all the
day, for I do not know their limits."
—Psalm 71:15

chapter thirteen

A Lesson in Sword Fighting

"And take the sword of the Spirit,
Which is the word of God.
—Ephesians 6:17

U sually when I get to the end of the armor of God, I'm feeling inspired. I am ready to head out to war and victory! Everything seems possible. I believe in the armor I'm wearing, and it's easy to feel invincible. But this is also where I often mess up. My attention span is short, and I feel bored and ready for action by the time I'm all suited up in my protective gear.

And so I go to battle without my weapon.

Oh, I trust in the Spirit to lead me. But my mistake is that I expect Him to do all the fighting *for* me as well. I tend to go along for the ride. Why not? I'm covered in armor from head to toe — and so going to battle becomes more like a sightseeing adventure than hand-to-hand combat.

If I do not learn to push my laziness and natural, self-indulgent tendencies aside, I will never be able to advance in this war God has called me to fight in along with all believers. It takes work to learn how to wield the sword of the Spirit. To an inexperienced swordsman, it can feel cumbersome and hard to handle. The devil loves to take advantage of this apparent weakness, and his deceptions are aimed at our hearts, ready to fire during our most vulnerable times.

My three-year-old has been sick with a painful auto-immune disease for 6 weeks now. I felt like I was handling it well until I noticed this victim mentality creeping in. Not a "Why me, my kid is sick" feeling, but a quickness to feel offended and attacked by those I love and who I know love me. It has thrown me into depression, and I find myself reaching for a weapon that is easier to handle than the Spirit's own sword. I look for sympathy, and I reward myself with simple amusements or simply sulk around, making life miserable for everyone around me.

When the Spirit convicts me and tells me to combat these selfish feelings with God's Word, I argue with Him. I have some really good arguments too. *Hurts can be God's way of speaking to us,* I reason. *God is allowing me to be tested and making me into His image,* I say. I'm smart in my arguments — just like the devil was smart in tempting me with deceptive feelings.

The truth is, if I don't combat these hurt feelings for what they are — vicious attacks from the enemy — they will take over my heart until I live in a constant state of depression. This is true for all of us. While you may be tempted in different areas than I am, the remedy remains the same for us all: rigorous training with the sword of the Spirit. Many athletes and dietitians recommend getting active, going for a run or working out, when we want to give in and binge on food that's not good for our bodies. The same principle works in our spiritual lives. When we face temptation, we need to combat it actively. Better yet, we need to make a spiritual workout a regular part of our day, purposely fighting temptations before they hit us.

How to train

In the old days, when a man wanted to become a knight, he would go through hours, days and months of training. Day in and day out he would train. Experienced instructors would test his strength and skill, and he would slowly advance up the ranks, finally attaining his goal after much work and unbelievable effort. It took grit and determination and a whole lot of stick-to-itiveness. Finally the day would arrive, and his achievements would be publicly applauded as, kneeling at his sovereign's feet, he became one of the king's knights.

God's ways are so often different than man's. He rescues us from our sins and immediately gives us a place in His army. We start off kneeling at His feet, and then He trains us in warfare. We can choose to embrace His training and throw ourselves into it with energy and determination, or we can slowly wallow along, going around and around in a cycle of small victories followed by temptation and defeat.

I don't know about you, but I don't have time for the latter! God has placed His precious children in my care, and if I can't lead them victoriously, their souls are in danger. And so I *must* choose to spend time training with God's own sword. There is no other choice. For me, this almost always happens at the expense of some other project, and it will most likely be the same way for you. We moms could work day and night and still not get everything done that we want to. And when we do manage to get some down time, we usually have plans on how we will spend it.

But there is a war going on all around us. Everywhere we turn we can see its effects and face another battle. Training with the sword isn't just a choice for victory — it is our only chance for survival.

We need to make it a habit to run to God's Word every single time we are tempted, but beyond that, we need to study His word constantly! It is not enough to just run for a sword when we see an enemy in the distance. We need to know how to use it *skillfully*. That means dwelling on it, studying it and developing a *love* for it. God's Word should always be our first line of defense. We need to practice using it until it becomes a part of ourselves.

It will take work. It isn't always fun. There are days when studying the Bible sounds dry and unappealing to me. I really want to sit down with a cup of coffee and drown my sorrows in my favorite Netflix show or social media. This isn't always bad, but it should always, *always* happen after we spend time with Jesus. Not because we need to become legalistic, but because Jesus is the greatest part of our existence. Without Him, we would be nothing. We would be lost and headed towards our just punishment. When we love someone, we need to listen to their heart. The Bible is the heart of God, written out for our benefit. Do we dare prioritize it above pleasures that will never last? Do we dare not to?

Handle with care

When we were kids, my one and only brother was fascinated with old weapons. He loved to create bows and arrows, using the methods Native Americans have used for years. Other times he would carve Bowie knives or swords out of wood. Being the closest in age to him out of five sisters, I would often get the benefits of his knowledge. We had many outdoor adventures together, and my tomboy antics caused my mom a little concern. I don't remember any particular sword fight, but I'm sure we had them and I know I learned that even a wooden sword can hurt and should be handled with care.

The Bible describes the sword of the Spirit as "living and powerful, and sharper than any two-edged sword, piercing even to the division of soul and spirit, and of joints and marrow...a discerner of the thoughts and intents of the heart" (Hebrews 4:12).

In other words, handle it with care! Our sword is created out of the words of God Himself. It is an ancient weapon, and yet it is as sharp and deadly as if He has just forged it in Heaven's flames. It is so powerful we will never learn the depths of it. The Word of God is the Spirit's own sword, and He wields it so skillfully as to separate soul from spirit. Clearly we need to do more than just fill our hearts with it. We need the Holy Spirit's touch so we can use it in a discerning way. If we use this sword as a weapon for our own advantage, we will wound those around us and even ourselves.

I am not saying this to scare anyone from using it. We need, and are even commanded, to use it and use it often. Yet so often we take the holy commands of God and, feeling completely equipped, run with them to our own destruction and the hurt of those around us. When we do not use the Word of God according to the Spirit's instruction, we easily twist our pet passages of Scripture to justify ourselves and judge others. This causes divisions and deep wounds that are not from Christ. Yes, we must live in faith, truth and righteousness, by the Word of God. But we must do so at the Spirit's instruction, or we will cause damage. These are not mere child's playthings, but the originals, created to destroy the enemy. We must wear our armor constantly and use the sword daily, but we must do it God's way, not ours.

If the devil cannot keep us from studying God's Word, he will probably try to make us prideful. He doesn't run out of temptations, and until we get to Heaven, we will not be completely out of his reach. If we make it our purpose to study and train in the Spirit's sword, the devil will most likely do his best to make us proud of our own accomplishments. It is a puzzle to me how I can walk away from a wonderful time with Jesus and immediately take credit for what I learned or throw my knowledge around at others, but it happens. And wounding others, even our children, with the Word of God is not something we want to be guilty of.

To put it practically, when my child embarrasses me in public by loud and blatant disobedience, I have a choice. I can angrily tell them what the Bible says about honoring parents or I can remember that Scripture also tells me that "A soft answer turns away wrath, but a harsh word stirs up anger" (Proverbs 15:1). Each response is putting the sword of the Spirit to use; the first in a hurtful way and the second in a wise way.

The Word of God is sharp and no matter what spirit we say things in, if we are quoting the Word of God there will be some truth to what we say because God's Word *is* truth. Yet it is not our job to prick others with the Spirit's sword. Yes, there are times when God may use us to speak a word of truth and conviction to a fellow warrior or our children, but this should be done by the Spirit's leading, with much grace and even a certain level of fear or reluctance

So all this to say: use the sword daily, by all means! But stay tuned to the Spirit and follow His lead. Fight the devil with all your might, but wound those around you with reluctance and only after much prayer.

Practical sword practice

I have read many articles on the armor of God, and I always feel inspired yet unsure. What next? How do I actually apply this practically, especially in this busy season of motherhood?

The blanket answer is to run to Jesus. He knows you and your personality. He knows your season and your struggles. He knows your *heart*, and He wants to help and walk every busy, messy step of parenting with you. He wants to be in the moment with you.

So first of all, invite Him to lead you. Ask Him to map out your days. Take your schedule and your to-do lists and lay them at His feet. Ask Him to show you how to arrange your days so that He is the priority. Center your days on Jesus, and you will find that things will work themselves out around *Him*. No, you will not always get everything done on your list. But if Jesus is your first priority, and the only thing of value you accomplish is spending time with Him, you can go to bed feeling good about your day. (Of course you need to take care of your family too.)

Jesus is creative. He never tells you that your quiet time needs to look just like your neighbor's, your best friend's or your favorite author or speaker's. He wants it to be a special time of you connecting with His spirit in an intimate way that is unique to you. And if you take all your concerns and excuses to Him, He will bring inspiration and show you how to spend time with Him. Not just enough time to survive, but to thrive. This doesn't necessarily mean three hours a day. It might mean 10-20 minutes in the morning and then a verse to ponder all day. Or it might mean something totally different. The most important thing is to bring a heart that is empty of others' expectations and rules and let Jesus fill it up in the way that best works for you and your season of life.

This is an exciting venture! We can't let fear or anything hold us back. God wants to train us in sword fighting, and all we need to bring is an open, humble heart. There are giants of doubt and deception to be slain — in our own lives and for our children. We are warriors; let's start our training today!

Do you feel skilled with the sword of the spirit? How are you lacking?

_____

_____

_____

_____

_____

Even the best swordsmen must continually practice. How can you add sword practice to your daily schedule? What would that look like for you?

_____

_____

_____

_____

_____

Take some time to think of the areas you're prone to be weak in spiritually. Find verses to defend those areas and add them to your daily practice time. Write the verses and/or references down here:

_____

_____

_____

_____

_____

"The Spirit of God worketh in, by, and through, and with the Word; and if we keep to that Word, we may rest assured that the Holy Ghost will keep with us, and make our testimony to be a thing of power."

—Charles Spurgeon[1]

chapter fourteen

Come Freely

"Praying always with all prayer and supplication in the
Spirit, being watchful to this end with all perseverance
And supplication for all the saints."
—Ephesians 6:18

S he woke up and slowly pulled herself to a sitting position. She
looked around her surroundings and smiled. It was a humble little
room to be sure, but it was hers.

She had moved in just yesterday, and the thrill was still in her heart. Her
own home! She was under nobody's authority — there was no one to
tell her what she could or could not do. Her heart swelled with gratitude
towards the Mayor of the city. It was to him she owed her thanks for her
own place.

She marveled at his generosity. All the young people in the town had
their own little set of rooms because of him. Whenever a young person
became old enough to live on their own, the Mayor had a little meeting
with them, and they would come to an arrangement. In exchange for
small services for himself and his city council, the Mayor would give
them their own place in his special apartments.

It was the perfect plan.

As the weeks went on, the young girl quickly fell into her new routine:
breakfast at the Mayor's sumptuous table every morning, checking to see
if he had any errands for her, and finishing her tasks. Then she was free

to do whatever she pleased. The Mayor provided everything she needed to be comfortable and happy. It was a good life.

Except for one thing.

A man standing on the street by the marketplace every day would always try to talk with the young people in the Mayor's employ. He never tried to stop them from their jobs, but simply wanted to talk with them. He was dirty, like he had traveled many miles. He was not particularly handsome, and there was nothing charismatic or exciting about him.

But that wasn't the problem the girl had with him. It was his words she did not like. He tried to convince the Mayor's young workers that their benefactor was not who they thought he was. The traveler told them that the Mayor was a trickster. He did not have their good at heart. In fact, he was evil.

And he was out to destroy them.

It made her laugh to hear the traveler talk. Did he really think she would believe him? It was the Mayor, after all, who gave her everything she had. Her home and her meals came from him, as well as her entertainment, for he was always bringing in great entertainers for the amusement of the people. He knew the way to a young person's heart.

The young girl took to slinging dirt and mud at the stranger, along with insults, just like all the other young people did. The Mayor kept threatening to do away with the man, and she wished he would. He was a nuisance and a pain.

When the Mayor finally did take action against the stranger, she was right there with the crowd, hurling insults, curses and stones. As the man crumpled lifeless to the ground, she laughed.

The next day, her life was changed.

With the threat of the stranger gone, the Mayor revealed his true self. He called a meeting and informed all of his "employees" that he was grateful for their loyalty in the past months, but it was time for them to know something: they were not free as he had led them to believe — they were his slaves, and they would never escape.

She didn't know she was a slave.

At first the girl resisted. But after beatings and poor treatment, her spirit soon broke and she gave in. For her rebellion she was kicked out onto the streets and banned from the Mayor's table, but still expected to run errands for the tyrant she belonged to. She was given many extra menial tasks, and she felt alone and overwhelmed. She was trapped — trapped in a life she had chosen for herself because she was deceived by the glamor of being her own boss. Now she had nothing.

And then it happened. One day as she sat begging by the gate, hoping for even the smallest morsel of food, he came back. The traveler. She knew him instantly, even though he looked nothing like he had when she had last seen him. He was alive. He was well dressed and riding a white charger. He was...a King.

Their eyes met, and she knew that he knew her too. His eyes pierced her soul, and she realized he could read her heart. She wanted to run, but couldn't. And where would she go anyway? She knew the mayor would kill her someday; why not just die at the hands of this strange man?

And then the Mayor came out of his palace, angry and afraid. He quailed before the stranger, but glared at the girl. "Get out of here. Now!" he screamed at her. She turned to run, hoping to avoid blows, when the words stopped her.

"She's mine."

She turned and stared. Her tormentor glared at the stranger. "You know the cost of a soul," he snarled. "It has been paid." The stranger replied quietly but with unmistakable authority. "My life, for hers."

Chills ran down the girl's back. *His* life? His *life?* She had helped throw the stones of death, yet he was willing to buy her back from this evil fiend who controlled her life? And, in her heart, she knew it was true. She knew *He* was true.

She was His.

She watched in amazement as he got off his horse, and the Mayor scuttled back to his palace in fear, screaming curses as he went. He walked up to her and wiped the mud off her face. He gave her a robe of the softest, most perfect white with his regal mark on it. He put a crown of pure gold on her head.

He placed his hand on her shoulder and called her...

His child.

The daughter of the King.

The royal privilege of prayer

This girl is me — and she is you. In our own ways we each lived in defiance of Jesus. We thought our way was better, and we resisted His gentle words of life. It was because of our sin that He died, and yet He calls us His daughters. He has washed us clean and given us a new life. And more than that, He takes joy in us! He cares for us in the most tender way.

> "The Lord has taken away your judgements, He has cast out your enemy. The King of Israel, the Lord, is in your midst; you shall see disaster no more...The Lord your God is in your midst, the Mighty One, will save; He will rejoice over you with gladness, He will quiet you with His love, He will rejoice over you with singing" (Zephaniah 3:15, 17).

If God's Kingdom was ruled in the way that earthly kingdoms are, we would spend the rest of our lives in misery. Even if we would by chance be favored by the King, we still would not be able to enter His presence freely and pour out our hearts at any given hour. Instead we would have to wait for His invitation or risk our lives as Esther did before her husband, the King of Persia.

But God is not like this. Instead of scorning our presence, He freely invites us to join Him in His royal throne room. "Let us therefore come boldly to the throne of grace, that we may obtain mercy and find grace to help in time of need" (Hebrews 4:16).

How do we enter the throne room of Heaven? By prayer. Prayer is a royal privilege we do not deserve, and yet it has been given to us. And what is more, God tells us over and over to use it continually. We cannot take advantage of God when it comes to prayer. We can never enter His presence too often. There is no royal scribe sitting at God's side, tallying the amount of times we entreat Him for help in one day. No one stands at the entrance with a big stick, saying "You've already been here five times today. God doesn't have time to talk to you again; come back tomorrow."

I don't know about you, but when my children come to me with request after request, I can quickly grow impatient. Like I want to say, "Give me some peace and quiet for just a few minutes, *please*!" But God is the perfect parent. He is love in its entirety, and He invites us to come as often as we please.

Because of our sin, we drove the nails into Jesus' hands, and yet we may now stand before Him as His beloved daughters. It is the crazy, unworldly mystery of grace.

Prayer glorifies God

As moms, we can be a daily example of wearing the armor of God well. We can teach our kids truth, talk about righteous living and give them opportunities to serve. We can show them what it looks like to choose faith over doubt, to live out our salvation and to expertly handle the sword of the Spirit. But we cannot *be* the Holy Spirit to them, and we cannot force them to follow Jesus.

And so our first and last line of defense should be prayer. In many ways, prayer takes our children out of our weak, human hands and places them into the ever capable hands of our Father, who knows them better than we ever could.

I spend so much time trying to figure out what it is that makes my children tick. I can see that the discipline that works well with my oldest is not effective with my middle child. With time, I learn that the love language of my son can be vastly different than my oldest daughter's. I am even beginning to see the different ways they think about and relate to God. But I still do not know them perfectly, and I never will. Even if I try to figure out the exact right way to train each one of them, I will still fail them in some ways.

Thankfully, God did not choose me to be their mother because He knew I would be a perfect mom. He chose me to parent my particular children because He knew it was the way in which I could glorify Him best. He chose me to parent them because He knew that they would send me straight to Him, desperately needy in the best way possible. He chose me for *His* purposes.

God wants to be glorified in our parenting, and the best way we can do that is to give it back to Him through prayer. Yes, we need to do our work faithfully, but it should always be sandwiched in prayer. We need to glorify God by acknowledging our imperfections and placing our children in His perfect care.

Intercessory prayer

When we were lost in our sins, we were on the path to an eternity without Jesus. But Jesus took our place and interceded for us when we could not defend ourselves. Now He calls us to do the same for those around us. In Ezekiel 22 God says that He sought for someone to stand in the gap on behalf of the land, but there was no one to be found.

This was heartbreaking because it meant that the land was lost. To stand in the gap means to place oneself in a gap or hole in a wall and fight off invaders in valiant hand-to-hand combat. To stand in the gap means to deliberately place yourself between a vulnerable person and the one who wishes to kill them.

There is a battle for each of our children's souls, and who better to stand in the gap for them than we ourselves? The devil is always looking for holes through which he can gain an advantage in their lives. As their moms, we probably know these holes better than anyone else. We were created to intercede for them, to stand in those holes and tell the devil that they are not his territory! We must fight for our children in passionate, wrestling prayer.

There is no time for rest and no chance for retreat. We need to remain vigilant, observing the weaknesses in our children's hearts and filling them in with fervent, unrelenting intercession to their Creator! At the same time, we need to strengthen the walls around their hearts before they have a chance to grow weak and vulnerable in different areas.

How do we do this? One way is to pray God's own words over them continually. When we pray Scripture over our children, it's like we are using a powerful, three-fold weapon on their behalf. We are unleashing truth, the sword of the Spirit and prayer, each full of might on their own. When used together the result can be nothing less than spectacular. This is intercession of the most powerful kind!

The Psalms are full of verses we can turn into prayers, and so are the epistles. In many of Paul's epistles, he shares how he is praying for the particular church he is writing to. David talks about how God has worked many marvelous things in his life throughout the Psalms. Pray those verses over your kids!

(In the appendix to this book, you'll find a list of Scripture prayers to use in intercession for your children.)

Don't forget your armor!

Don't grow impatient waiting for God to answer your prayers. He is not hasty, and He is never late. You may not see the answers to your prayers when you think you should, but you can rest in the fact that He has heard and He will answer. The devil will use every tactic he can to get you to doubt God and the power of heartfelt, humble prayers. This is why God gave you armor and a sword. Don't forget to use them.

And remember, even though your prayers may at times be feeble and undiscernible, even though your heart may feel broken from the weight of them, God hears and understands. He has given us this promise, "Likewise the Spirit also helps in our weaknesses. For we do not know what we should pray for as we ought, but the Spirit Himself makes intercession for us with groanings which cannot be uttered" (Romans 8:26).

You can take every burden and care of your heart to Him, and He will hear you and give you an answer that will ultimately bring glory to Him and inspire worship in your heart.

When we put all of our armor to use, great things will happen in the Kingdom of God. Victories will be won, and "'no weapon that is formed against you shall prosper, and every tongue which rises against you in judgement you shall condemn. This is the heritage of the servants of the Lord, and their righteousness is from me,' says the Lord" (Isaiah 54:17 NKJV).

Our heritage is one of victory! Not because we are strong or do everything right, but because we belong to Jesus and He is the ultimate Victor. And He tells us that when we use His weapons, we will pull down strongholds and cast down arguments and all things that exalt themselves above the knowledge of God (2 Corinthians 10:3-5).

Moms have a great influence over their kids and the kind of people they will become. As moms who have free entrance to the throne room of heaven, our impact can be greater than we ever imagined. Let us come freely before His throne and continually intercede on their behalf. Their futures depend on it!

Is prayer a last resort or first line of defense for you, particularly in raising your children?

_____

_____

_____

No matter your answer to the above, what practical steps can you take to make it better? How can you set aside more time or add strength to your prayers?

_____

_____

_____

_____

_____

"Until you believe that life is war, you cannot know what prayer is for. Prayer is for the accomplishment of a wartime mission."

—John Piper[1]

chapter fifteen

The Greatest Of All

"The greatest of these is love."
—1 Corinthians 13:13

My sister has a talent for making friends. She has made friends at the park and in the library and probably a lot of other places I haven't heard about yet. Her personality is this perfect mix of bubbly and fearless that I often find myself envying. A friend of mine is a sweet, servant-hearted person. She is always willing to willing to work in the hidden places, sharing her love for others by acts of service. Yet another friend has faith that truly can move mountains. Every time I spend time with her, I walk away in amazement. Oh, to have faith like that!

Each friend I spend time with ignites this desire in my heart to possess some part of their gifting. I'm not the only one who does this, am I? I think we all have a friend or two (or ten) that we can learn from and whose gifts we sometimes envy. Paul talked about this in 1 Corinthians 12 as he explained spiritual gifts. He tells us that everyone has their own God-given gift, and we should appreciate and learn from each other's gifts and talents. He also encourages us to earnestly desire the best gifts.

"And yet," he says, "there is an even better way, and I'll show it to you right now." Then he launches into one of his most poetic and well-known chapters ever. It's easy to skim over 1 Corinthians 13 because we have heard it *so many times*. We read it on signs and mugs and hear it preached over the pulpit. Sometimes, I like to think of what it would sound like if Paul were speaking directly to moms sitting in my living room. Not because Scripture ever gets stale and needs to be rewritten, but because sometimes my attitude needs an adjustment. And so if I were face to face with Paul, and he had time to expound a little, I think 1 Corinthians 13 might have sounded a little bit like this:

Even if I have been divinely gifted to speak every language known to mankind so that I might preach the gospel to every tribe, tongue and nation, but don't have love, I might as well be screaming "bla bla bla" into everyone's ear while pounding on a drum. And even if God gifted me with the ability to speak the language of heavenly beings, so that I could praise Him with the same words as those who surround His throne, but I have no love in my heart or loving actions for the people He has placed in my life, I might as well be jamming out with my headphones and a loud set of cymbals. It would mean absolutely nothing to anyone around me.

God could give me the ability to tell the world what the future holds. He could gift me with wisdom and knowledge beyond my years so that thousands would line up to hear me speak, but if I don't love my family with His perfect love, I might as well be the most unknown person in the world. Because my work counts for nothing if it is not done in love.

If I have the greatest faith ever seen, so that I can literally move Mount Everest into any ocean I choose, but do not have divine love, I am absolutely nothing. I could give every one of my possessions away and even offer up my life for another and yet, if I do it out of a selfish drive for a good reputation, and not because of the love of Jesus, it will not do me one bit of good. After all, it was love that beckoned Jesus to the cross, not a search for popularity.

True love, the love Jesus pours into a mother's heart, will patiently serve throughout long hours that turn into days, weeks, months and years, completely unnoticed and unseen by anyone the world thinks important. God's love is kind, even when the days are long and nothing goes right. God's love enables me to speak gently to my child when I'd rather scream at what they just did. Love does not long for the things that others have because it has learned to be content in the sweet gifts God has already given. Love brings contentment.

God-given love does not put itself on parade. It doesn't parent for the good opinion of those who may be watching, but rather for the glory of God and the good of our children, even in the most difficult and trying of moments. Love from God does not seek glory from others so that it can exult in itself. True love is polite and considerate of those around it, including children. It teaches children how to treat others through example rather than by repeating the same words over and over again. True love in a mother's heart will cause her to seek the good of her family above her own comforts. It means saying "no" to excessive self-care and "me-time."

A heart of love will give patience to a mom right in the middle of severe provocation, like when your child pitches a fit at Wal-Mart or spills your morning coffee on your lap before you've had one sip. A mind that is controlled by Divine Love will not jump to evil conclusions and will always look for the best in every family member and friend.

You may have been wounded, but if you give yourself over to Jesus and accept His love, you will never rejoice to see bad things happen to those who have hurt you or made your life miserable. Truth is what will make you happy, and as you are filled with love, you will be able to see truth clearly in all situations.

A love-filled heart willingly bears the burdens of life, knowing each one was handpicked by the Creator of Love itself. A mom who has a heart of love has hope because she knows that as much as she loves her child, Jesus loves him more and that hope makes all things possible. She will endure heartache, ridicule and postponements to her most cherished longings because she trusts in the perfect love of her Savior.

Love can never ever fail. It will always triumph, no matter the circumstances. I may prophecy or speak many languages, even celestial ones, but one day that will end. I may be full of knowledge and even wisdom, but one day it too will vanish, like clouds after a storm. Our knowledge and our prophecies will never be perfect because we are only human, but perfect love will last forever, even after knowledge and prophesying are gone and the world is no more.

There was a time when, as a child, I said, did and thought childish things. My understanding was incomplete, and I didn't even know it. But as I grew older and more mature, I began to see and understand life and reality more completely and clearly. And my spiritual life is no different. I feel like I know so much more than I did about following Jesus and using my gifts for His glory, but the growth of a spiritual heart never stops. I actually know only a small part of what there is to know, no matter what spiritual gifts God has given me. But a day is coming when I shall see everything clearly, and then I will know myself as Jesus, the One who created me, knows me now. Then I will understand exactly why He gave me the gifts He did.

Until then, I know that faith, hope and love will last forever, and I should earnestly pursue all three, but above all, I should desire perfect love.

Two kinds of love

Honestly, when I read what the Bible has to say about love, and even as I write these words, I feel condemnation piling up in my heart. I remember the hasty, grouchy words that flew out of my mouth when my five-year-old spilled my coffee after a particularly difficult morning.

I remember the times I selfishly told my kids to go play because I wanted a little more time to browse social media. So many times I have failed in my parenting. It's not easy to always choose to love, to give, to serve and to do it all *cheerfully*. But this is the good thing. Paul wasn't talking about human love. He was talking about *divine love*. Love that goes so far beyond human reasoning that it is impossible for our finite minds to fathom.

There are two different kinds of love in the Bible, and both are important. There is the love that is a deliberate choice. There are many commands in the Bible directing us to love one another. In fact, when Jesus quoted the two greatest commandments, they were both about love.

> "Jesus said to him, 'You shall love the Lord your God with all your heart, with all your soul, and with all your mind.' This is the first and great commandment. And the second is like it: 'You shall love your neighbor as yourself.' On these two commandments hang all the Law and the Prophets" (Matthew 22:37-40).

Sometimes choosing to love feels like walking on a rock-filled path barefoot. It is hard, and it can hurt our tender feelings to turn the other cheek and allow others to think wrong of us or poke fun at us. It is painful to continue walking in love when those around us are deliberately filling the path with stones. But it is a choice we must make nonetheless. This is the first kind of love and the first step we need to take towards divine love.

1 Corinthians 13 takes love a step further and explains the ins and outs of divine, Christ-given love in great detail. Divine love is love with shoes on.

Not my love

1 Corinthians 13 isn't about trying and trying, hoping to one day reach perfection while praying all the while that it won't be too late. It's not

about begging God to not let our imperfections ruin our children forever. It's much bigger and goes far beyond our own efforts. It is not our own love at all, but the love of Jesus flowing through us.

The love described in 1 Corinthians 13 is about falling into the love of Jesus ourselves. It is about connecting with *Him*, so that our love is not our own but *His*. The truth is, we cannot love our children as described above. But instead of depressing us, this should make us do a happy dance through the kitchen! Our children can grow up with a love that goes deeper than even the love of a mother; they can grow up with the perfect love of Jesus. When we open our hearts to let Jesus pour His perfect love over our hurts and imperfections, it will run over our walls like a waterfall. The walls we have built around our hearts over time, the walls we trust to protect us, will come crashing down so that the love of Jesus will pour through us and out onto our children, unhindered and beautiful.

Because we are human, we fail to love our children perfectly through our own efforts, yet the love of Jesus works inside us. We can let go of the stress of striving to be the perfect mom and instead run to Jesus, allowing Him to shape us into the mom He created us to be. We can trust the love of Jesus to flow through us into our apologies when we mess up. We can trust the love of Jesus to smooth the rough edges of our parenting.

This doesn't mean we can parent however we want and expect love to erase the bad and enhance the good. Love doesn't work like Photoshop or an Instagram filter. It is much stronger and changes us from the inside out. When we truly give ourselves over to the love of Jesus, our parenting will change. We won't be able to help it. Our patience will grow, and kindness will come more naturally.

Divine love is a seed that Jesus planted in our hearts when we first turned to Him and asked Him to take us as His own. We can choose to love, and the Bible commands us to. Part of love is a choice we make day in and day out. We have to choose to stick with it and love over the difficult seasons and days of parenting. But when we choose to love like Jesus, His divine love takes control of our hearts. We can't make divine love grow any more than we can make a oak tree grow from an acorn. But we can cultivate it by spending time with Jesus and in His Word. We can water it and feed it, and then God will cause it to grow and increase in the way He knows will be best.

On days when we are struggling to love well, we can run to Jesus and ask Him to show Himself strong on our behalf. And soon we will be rejoicing in His strength, just as Paul did. "But He said to me, 'My grace is sufficient for you, for my power is made perfect in weakness,' therefore I will boast all the more gladly of my weaknesses, so that the power of Christ may rest on me'" (2 Corinthians 12:9).

Love isn't a burden to be borne or a battle to be fought. It is a gift our Creator has freely given to us. Freely we have received, freely may we give.

Is it easy for you to receive the gift of love?

_____

Why or why not?

_____
_____
_____
_____

How can you deliberately choose to love your children today?

_____
_____
_____
_____

How can you cultivate divine love on a daily basis?

_____

_____

_____

_____

_____

_____

_____

"If I live to be loved more than to love, then I know nothing of
Calvary's love."
—Amy Carmichael[1]

chapter sixteen

Run to Jesus

"The Lord is my Rock and my Fortress and my
Deliverer; the God of my strength, in Whom
I will trust; My shield and the Horn of my Salvation,
My Stronghold and my Refuge."
—2 Samuel 22:2-3

I could say so much more about each subject we covered in this book. I could go on, trying to capture everything it means to be a warrior mom and putting it into words, but I could never do it justice. I hope and pray my words have ignited a spark in your heart that will grow into a roaring flame and a drive to honor God in every aspect of parenting so that you can stand before Him and say, "Everything I've done has been for *You*, my Lord!" And I hope you'll hear Him reply, "Well done, good and faithful servant!"

We can sum up being a warrior mom very simply. Run to Jesus, our Tower of Refuge. This is where every battle should be fought from. A soldier fighting from a fortress always has a huge advantage. All the knowledge and Christian learning in the world could never equip us to fight against the Prince of Darkness. We have no choice but to run to Jesus every time there is a battle to be fought.

Jesus wants to fight for us and by our side. Let's go back to 2 Samuel 22. We touched on it in chapter five, but I want to cover it a little more in depth. In this Psalm, David recounts the mighty things God did on his behalf before he was finally crowned king. When I read it as it applies to spiritual warfare, I get chills. God is *for* us! It is absolutely incredible.

When we call to God to help us in moments of overwhelm and defeat, He literally shakes heaven and earth to come to our aid. Listen to how David vividly describes it:

"In my distress I called upon the Lord, and cried out to my God; He heard my voice from His temple, and my cry entered His ears. Then the earth shook and trembled; the foundations of heaven quaked and were shaken, because He was angry...The Lord thundered from heaven and the Most High uttered His voice. He set out arrows and scattered them; lighting bolts, and He vanquished them" (2 Samuel 22:7, 8, 14 & 15).

We can use willpower and make elaborate plans, but the truth is, if we don't ask God to help us, we cannot win. We need God's strength for everything, from the small skirmishes to the biggest battle we ever face. We do not need to hesitate to call for His help either because He delights in us just as we delight in our own children.

"He also brought me out into a broad place; He delivered me because He delighted in me" (2 Samuel 22:20).

But God doesn't stop with just helping us out of calamities. He lights our path, shows us which way to walk, and He Himself teaches us how to battle. He wants us to grow strong in Him, and He doesn't just sit back and wait for it to happen. He becomes our personal trainer, showing us how put on our armor, how to fight, and giving us more strength than we knew was possible.

"For You are my lamp O Lord; the Lord shall enlighten my darkness. For by You I can run against a troop; by my God I can leap over a wall...God is my strength and power, and He makes my way perfect...He teaches my hands to make war, so that my arms can bend a bow of bronze. You have also given me the shield of Your salvation; Your gentleness has made me great" (2 Samuel 22:29, 30, 33, 35 & 36).

Finding balance

There is a delicate balance in fighting this holy war. We can do *nothing* without the grace and strength of God. We know this, and yet neither can we sit and twiddle our thumbs, hoping it will all turn out right in the end. We have to decide we *will* do right and engage our discipline and will to follow the way of Christ no matter what. It takes deliberate purpose to raise our children for Christ. Paul says it so well:

> "Therefore I run thus: not with uncertainty. Thus I fight: not as one who beats the air. But I discipline my body and bring it into subjection, lest, when I have preached to others, I myself should become disqualified" (1 Corinthians 9:26-27).

How do we find this balance without tumbling off the tightrope to either side? By running to Jesus! Satan will trip us up in any way he can, and he never stops. Even while we may be winning the victory in one area, he will take that victory and appeal to our pride. We can never run to Jesus too often or too soon.

I have started audibly asking Jesus to help me, right in the middle of a situation. There are times when I run to my room and get on my knees, but this isn't always possible. So when the kids are fighting or a glass of milk spills all over the table while a plate full of food gets knocked to the floor, I just say it right out loud: "Oh Jesus, please help me and strengthen me! I need you now, Lord!"

I have found this to be powerful in so many different ways. First, it stops me in my tracks and reminds me that a plateful of spaghetti on the floor isn't going to keep anyone from Heaven. Second, it shows my kids that we can run to Jesus at any time and in any place. Third, this tells the devil he is not going to win this time. The battle is won the instant we pass it out of our incapable hands into the victorious, nail-scarred hands of our Savior.

So be disciplined and fight hard. But above all, run to Jesus at the first sign of battle, as if your life depends on it. Fight from the shelter of His tower of refuge. It is the only place you will find peace, safety and victory.

The world tells us so many things about who we need to be. But the world's opinion doesn't matter. We may never be a crafty mom or an Instagram mom or a perfectly dressed mom or even a perfectly calm and serene mom. But we can be a run-to-Jesus mom, and *that's* what counts. That is how we become a warrior mom.

Fight hard, friend. I'm cheering you on!

"The night is far spent, the day is at hand. Therefore let us cast off the works of darkness, and let us put on the armor of light."
—Romans 13:12

Appendix

Scripture Prayers

"Lord, may my child know that Your laws are true and righteous. May he find your words to be more desirable than gold and sweeter than honey. I ask that Your words will warn him of evil and that he will find great joy in keeping Your commands and ways."
Based on Psalm 19:9-11

"Lord, may my child choose wisdom and knowledge over riches. May she always choose Your words over anything the world offers. Your word says that the fear of the Lord is to hate evil, pride, arrogance and an all-knowing attitude. Fill her with a holy reverence and fear of You, Jesus!"
Based on Proverbs 8:10-13

"God, you are the glorious Father of our Lord Jesus Christ. All things are possible through You. I pray that You will give my child spiritual wisdom and understanding, so that he may grow in his knowledge of You. I pray his heart will be flooded with Light so he can understand the wonderful future You have promised to those You have called. Help him to realize what a rich and glorious future You have given to Your people! Let him understand the incredible greatness of Your power for all of us that believe on You."
Based on Ephesians 1:16-19

"Jesus, may my child be filled with the knowledge of Your will with all wisdom of spiritual understanding. May she always walk worthy of You, Lord, always pleasing You and being fruitful in every good work, increasing and growing in her knowledge of You. Strengthen my child in Your might, according to Your glorious power. Strengthen her in patience and long-suffering, with joyfulness."
Based on Colossians 1:9-11

"Lord, I pray that my child will have a hunger and thirst for Your word. May he seek after it and delight himself in its abundance. May he tune his ear to hear Your word and receive it."
Based on Isaiah 55:2

"Lord, may my child shun the wrong paths and influences. Give her a heart that delights in Your word. Make her as strong as a tree growing by a mighty river. May she be righteous and known by You."
Based on Psalm 1

"Lead my child in Your righteousness, Jesus. Make Your way straight before him. Cause my child to take refuge in You and be glad; let him ever sing for joy. Spread Your protection over him and cause him to rejoice in You. Bless him and surround him with Your favor as with a shield."
Based on Psalm 5

"Lord, open my child's eyes to see Your majesty and glory! Through the praise of children and infants You have established a stronghold against Your enemies. Use my child for Your glory and in Your Kingdom, Lord. Give me wisdom and guidance as I raise her to glorify You."
Based on Psalm 8

"Father, may my child never be ashamed of the gospel of Jesus Christ. Teach him the power of it, through You. Your righteousness is revealed in Your salvation. Fill him with an awe and a love for it and a sound, strong faith in it."
Based on Romans 1:16-17

"Jesus, I ask that my child's love of You may grow more and more and may they grow in knowledge and discernment because of it. This way they will know how to approve and accept the things that are excellent, this way they will be sincere and without offense till the day of Christ. May they be filled with the fruits of righteousness which are by Jesus Christ, to the glory and praise of God."
Based on Philippians 1:9-11

"Lord, I pray for my child, that You would count her worthy of the calling of Christ. May she fulfill your will and walk in Your goodness with faith and power. May the name of Jesus Christ be glorified in her and she in Him, according to the grace of our God and the Lord Jesus Christ."
Based on 2 Thessalonians 1:11-12

"Lord, may my child trust in Your mercy. Cause his heart to rejoice in Your salvation. May he sing praises to You forever because You have dealt generously with him."

Based on Psalm 13:5-6

"Father, I ask that You Yourself would train my child's hands for war. Show her Your lovingkindness and be her fortress and her Deliverer."

Based on Psalm 144:1-2

Acknowledgements

Virgil, there would be no book if it weren't for you. Thank you for your support, for being the first to read each chapter, for encouraging me and being completely amazing. I'm so grateful I get to parent with you. I love you so much.

Thank you Mom, for cheering me on! You are a wonderful example and I'm so thankful God made you my mom.

Thanks to my sisters, Kyla, Tara, Tori and Kirsten, for the love and support. I'm so glad we're family.

Thanks to my friends, Nyssa and Elicia for offering insight and encouragement throughout the entire book writing journey. You all are awesome!

Special thanks to my wonderful editor, Betsy DeCruz. It was an absolute joy to work with you and I appreciate your wisdom, advice and prayers.

A big thank you to Amy Kirk for capturing my vision so perfectly with your beautiful art. Your talent is inspiring!

Thank you to Jen Stults for creating the perfect book cover. I couldn't be happier with it!

Notes

Chapter 1: Broken for a Purpose
1. "The Complete Works of C. H. Spurgeon, Volume 38", p.707, Delmarva Publications, Inc
Chapter 2: Walking in Obedience
1. "Day by Day with C. H. Spurgeon," page 135, Kregel Classics

Chapter 3: Living in Joy
1. "I Come Quietly to Meet You: An Intimate Journey in God's Presence", p.79, Bethany House

Chapter 4: Mistaken Identity
1. "Strengthening Medicine for God's Servants" in The Metropolitan Tabernacle Pulpit Sermons (vol. 21; London: Passmore & Alabaster, 1875, 52–53"

Chapter 5: Mending the Holes
1. "Devotional Classics of C.H. Spurgeon," page 23, Sovereign Grace Publishers, inc.
2. https://www.merriam-webster.com/dictionary/warrior
3. "The complete works of C. H. Spurgeon," Volume 34: Sermons -Delmarva Publishing

Chapter 7: Entering the Battlefield
1. My Utmost for His Highest, May 5 - Barbour Books
2. "Devotional Classics of C. H. Spurgeon," August 24 - Sovereign Grace Publishers

Chapter 8: Putting on Truth
1. https://www.heartlight.org/spurgeon/1111-pm.html
Chapter 11: Defending with Faith
1. Hind's Feet on High Places – Page 83 – emphasis mine

Chapter 13: A Lesson in Sword Fighting
1.   Sermon   #2201,
https://www.blueletterbible.org/Comm/spurgeon_charles/sermons/2201.cfm?a=1103016

Chapter 14: Come Freely
1. John Piper

Chapter 15: The Greatest of All
1.   http://womenofchristianity.com/if-part-2-calvary-love-by-amy-carmichael/

About the Author

Stefani is passionate about serving Jesus in the big & little moments of everyday life. She loves to encouraging women to parent with purpose and passion. She and her husband, Virgil, have been married for six years and are busy raising their three kids close to the Rocky Mountains. She writes at wallsofhome.com and is the creator of the TruthBytes for Moms devotional app.